WEI-CHUAN'S COOKING SCHOOL was founded in 1961 as a subsidiary of the Wei-Chuan Food Corporation. This was a natural outgrowth from Wei-Chuan Foods since that corporation was the largest food manufacturer in Taiwan.

Wei-Chuan's Cooking school soon became the largest and most respected school of its kind in the Asia-Pacific rim. Graduates include world-class chefs, institutional teachers, professional caterers, connoisseurs of Chinese cuisine as well as many homemakers.

As Wei-Chuan's reputation grew, requests came from all over the world for guidance and information relative to the recipes used in the cooking classes. In an effort to meet this demand, CHINESE CUISINE was written and published in 1972. The book was very successful and became the first in a series of Wei-Chuan's Cookbooks. Wei-Chuan Publishing was founded later that same year in Taipei, with a branch subsequently established in the United States of America in 1978.

Wei-Chuan Cookbooks are recognized as the most comprehensive books on Chinese cuisine . They cover Chinese cooking, flower arrangements, microwave, garnishes, and healthful recipes.

Wei-Chuan's success can be attributed to its commitment to provide the best quality product possible. Every effort is made to include a color photograph with almost every recipe. The recipes are written simply with easy-to-follow instructions and precisely measured ingredients.

Wei-Chuan's future plans include an expansion of the types of cuisine offered through its cookbooks. Wei-Chuan stands behind its name, reputation , and commitment to remain true to the authenticity of the cuisine.

序 我從事中國烹飪研究及著作食譜至今已二十年，深得海內外讀者的愛顧。有鑒於現代人生活的忙碌及廚房設備的日新月異，促發了我再接再勵出版一本更能配合現代人生活步調的實用食譜。從來大家都認為做中國菜手續繁多，刀工、火候亦難掌握，費時費事而畏於嘗試，因此我著作本書的初衷即是要將中國菜現代化，走出中國炒鍋的窠臼，使人人都能做出簡單又可口的中國菜。

這本食譜中都是使用一般超市常見的材料，配上自製的中國式調味醬、汁，利用家庭常備的廚具，如烤箱、微波爐、電氣爐、不黏鍋……等，就可在短時間內做出道道可口的中國菜，不論熟手或初學者都能得心應手。

此書共集有 150 道家庭實用的簡易食譜及 50 餘種調味醬、汁，希望讀者們慢慢體會加以變換運用，我們更建議您選擇幾種喜愛的調味醬、汁，經常保存在冰箱內，則做菜時僅需花極少的時間就能滿足您一家的口腹，並保持您廚房的整潔。

此書在策劃、製作中均承蒙前味全烹飪學校校長黃淑惠女士的指導與協助，並得工作同仁的支持，使本書能順利完成，在此向大家致上我誠摯的謝意。

我寫這本書希望讓大家分享我的經驗，並謹以此書獻給我親愛的妻子 —— 優子，希望這本書能幫助她做個快樂的家庭主婦，並祝她永遠健康快樂。

INTRODUCTION

During the past 20 years I have devoted myself to developing Chinese cooking and writing Chinese cookbooks. The response from the readers in Taiwan and overseas is rewarding. CHINESE COOKING MADE EASY is published as a practical cookbook utilizing kitchen appliances not usually associated with the preparation of Chinese cuisine.

Many people are reluctant to cook Chinese food because they think it is complicated to prepare and too time consuming. The purpose of this book is to modernize Chinese cooking and make it easy. Alternative cooking equipment may be used as a substitute for the wok to simplify the preparation of the recipes.

This book will also help the reader learn how to make homemade Chinese style sauces. Ingredients readily available in supermarkets are utilized and the oven, microwave, non-stick pan, etc. are used to cook Chinese food. It is my hope that this book will encourage reluctant cooks and food lovers to prepare delicious meals.

There are 150 practical and easy to prepare home style recipes and more than 50 kinds of Chinese sauces and dressings. Readers may wish to switch the sauces and dressings to create new dishes. It is recommended that the sauces and dressings be stored in the refrigerator to save time in preparing dishes.

I would like to acknowledge and express my appreciation to all who have contributed to this book. To the previous director of Wei-Chuan's Cooking School, Su-Huei Huang, for her instruction and guidance throughout the years. To her colleagues, for their support and assistance in making this book a reality.

CHINESE COOKING MADE EASY was written to share my 20 years of Chinese cooking experience with the readers. It is my hope that this book will expand the reader's enjoyment of Chinese cuisine.

Finally, I dedicate this book to my wife in gratitude for her understanding and support in all my endeavors.

生於民國 39 年台灣省台北縣。現旅居夏威夷。
曾任味全烹飪學校教師　台灣中華電視台中國菜示範
美國味全烹飪學校教師　美國 NEW MEIJI 連鎖快餐公司指導
日本調理師學校中國料理主任教授　日本李魚翅海鮮中國菜館主理

Mr. Lee was born in Taipei. Taiwan and currently lives in Hawaii.
Mr. Lee's experience includes:
Master chef of "Lee's Garden Seafood Chinese Restaurant" in Japan.
Consultant for the "New Meiji" fast food chain stores in the United States.
Instructor: Wei-Chuan's Cooking School in the United States.
　　　　　Taiwan cooking classes on "Chinese Television Service".
　　　　　Wei-Chuan's Cooking School in Taipei.

李木村　Michael M.T. Lee

中國菜現代化 中國菜一向被認為是食的最高境界，不但是享受，更被譽為是吃的藝術。

　　所謂中國菜現代化，就是將傳統日常四菜一湯，有魚、有肉的組合簡化為由肉、海鮮、豆、蛋、奶類選一或混合，可如西餐按每人份分盛盤內，再配以蔬果及米飯，麵或麵包；或可再加湯、點心等。另外魚、肉類的處理儘量簡化，肉切絲、切片改為切大塊或整塊使用，並一次處理較多的份量調好味後分裝冷凍，隨時取用。如使用不黏鍋、烤箱、微波爐等新式廚具，更可方便善後清理。再加上本書內 50 餘種自製醬汁，相信讀者們都能在忙碌的生活中做出省時又好吃的中國菜。

MODERNIZED CHINESE COOKING Chinese cuisine is highly regarded by many food aficionados. Partaking of Chinese food is an enjoyable experience and it's preparation can be considered an art.

　　Traditionally, a Chinese meal consists of four different dishes and a soup. However, in modernizing and symplifying its presentation, Chinese cuisine now may be served in one main dish. Meat, seafood, beans, or eggs, individually or in combination, may be served as a main dish. Choose your favorite vegetables to accompany and complement the main dish then serve with rice, noodles, or bread. Fish and meat preparation may be simplified by cutting in large pieces or leaving them whole instead of shredding and slicing, or preparing in large quantities then refrigerating excess portions in containers for future use. In addition, using the simple sauces and dressings introduced in this book, a non-stick pan, oven, or a microwave, will contribute greatly to conserving time before and after you enjoy your Chinese cuisine.

　　Following the suggestions in this book, readers may find cooking delicious Chinese cuisine in a busy daily schedule is possible and enjoyable.

1

目錄 Table of Contents

換算表　Conversion Table

1杯（1飯碗）
1 cup (1 c.)= 236 c.c.

1大匙（1湯匙）
1 Tablespoon (1 T.)= 15 c.c.

1小匙（1茶匙）
1 teaspoon (1 t.)= 5 c.c.

1 磅＝16 盎司＝450 公克　　1 盎司＝28 公克
1 lb.=16 oz.=450 g　　　　　1 oz.=28 g

特殊材料說明
Descriptions for Some Special Ingredients and Sauces

1 黃芥末醬 （圖左）芥末粉 1 大匙加溫水 $\frac{3}{4}$ 大匙調勻後蓋緊，置 10 分鐘即成，色黃味辣。芥末粉係芥荣籽磨成的粉。

綠芥末醬 （圖右）有粉末及醬兩種，是薢荣根部磨碎製成，可與黃芥末醬交替使用。

2 辣豆瓣醬 是用辣椒加豆瓣釀製而成，味辣，本書使用之辣豆瓣醬（圖右）亦可用辣椒醬（圖左）代替。

3 甜麵醬 蒸熟麵糰醱酵製成，色黑。

海鮮醬 甜麵醬加工製成。

4 蘋果醋 用蘋果釀製而成，含果香，很適於涼拌蔬果類。

5 豆豉 將烏豆蒸熟再經醱酵加鹽水釀製，色黑味鹹甘。

6 乾辣椒 新鮮辣椒晒乾即成。

7 滷汁香料袋 （圖上）袋內材料與五香粉大同小異，但用原材料不研磨成粉。

五香粉 （圖下）將八角、花椒、桂皮、小茴香、三奈等多種香料炒香後磨成的粉。

8 八角 （圖左）形似六～八角星型而名之，又稱大茴香，產在中國南部，是中國菜常用香料之一種。

花椒 （圖右）又名山椒或川椒，是中國菜常用香料之一種。

花椒粉 將花椒炒香後壓碎成粉。

椒鹽 鹽 1 大匙炒熱拌上花椒粉半小匙即成。

1 **Yellow Mustard Sauce** (left side) is made by mixing 1 T. dry mustard with ³/₄ T. warm water; cover and let stand for 10 minutes. The sauce is yellow and becomes spicy. Dry mustard is made from finely crushed seeds of mustard green.

Green Mustard Sauce (right side) is made by mashing roots of horseradish and is available in powder or sauce form. It may also be used with yellow mustard sauce.

2 **Hot Bean Paste** is made by mixing bean paste with chili paste. Chili paste may be substituted for hot bean paste.

3 **Sweet Bean Paste** is made from fermented steamed bread. It is black and very thick.
Hoisin Sauce is made from Sweet Bean Paste.

4 **Apple Cider Vinegar** is made from apples and the flavor is suitable for mixing with cold fruit and vegetable dishes.

5 **Fermented Black Beans** are made by cooking, fermenting and then marinating black beans in salt water. The beans are black and taste salty.

6 **Dried Hot Red Pepper** is made by drying fresh hot red peppers.

7 **Spice Pouch** (upper side) contains the same basic ingredients as five-spice powder except the ingredients are in their original form.

Five-spice powder (lower side) is a combination of star anise, Szechuan peppercorns, cinnamon, fennel, and cloves that have first been stir-fried until fragrant and then ground to a fine powder.

8 **Star Anise** (left side) is a fragrant spice used often in Chinese cooking.

Szechuan Peppercorns (right side) is a spice used often in preparing Szechuan-style dishes.

Szechuan Peppercorn Powder is made from Szechuan peppercorns that have been stir-fried until fragrant and then ground to a fine powder.

Szechuan Peppercorn Salt is made by stir-frying 1 T. salt in a pan until the salt is very hot; mix it with ¹/₂ t. Szechuan peppercorn powder.

9 醬油 用黃豆或黑豆蒸熟醱酵加鹽、水調製而成；分深色（老抽）、淡色（生抽）、普通色三種，如無特殊說明，使用普通醬油即可。

10 蠔油 生蠔醱酵加鹽水調製而成，有特殊海鮮美味。

11 麻油 （圖上）用白或黑芝麻經烤或蒸後榨油製成，高級品色淡味香醇。

辣油 （圖下）辣椒粉加少許水拌濕，倒入燒熱蔬菜油待涼即成，市面有現成出售。

12 沙茶醬 各種辛香料磨碎調製而成，味香醇稍辣，一般買現成使用。

13 海菜類 海帶或海草乾燥品，泡水 10 分鐘至軟後使用。

14 鰹魚片 鰹魚蒸熟醱酵後曬乾再切薄片，東方食品部有售。高級品（圖右）撒在材料上配食，普通品（圖左）熬湯用。

15 米粉 （圖左）米的澱粉加工製成。

粉絲 （圖右）綠豆澱粉製成，又名細粉或冬粉。用水泡軟後使用。

16 香菇 （圖上）栽培在木頭上的菇類。香菇包括冬菇、北菇及花菇。使用時用溫水泡軟洗淨。

木耳 （圖下）生長在朽木上的菌類，因其形狀類似耳朵故稱木耳，使用時用水泡軟洗淨。

鷄湯 鷄骨或鷄肉加水（約 1：4 倍）小火煮 1～2 小時，市面有售鷄湯罐使用簡便。

麵包粉 白土司麵包切除表面黃皮，略晾乾（1～2 小時），再用手撕成小片，放入果汁機內攪碎，少量效果較好，市面有售現成，使用方便。

9 Soy Sauce is made by mixing steamed, fermented soybeans and black beans with salt and water. There are three kinds of soy sauce: dark, light, and regular soy sauce. Unless specified in the recipe, regular soy sauce should be used.

10 Oyster Sauce is made by mixing fermented oyster with water and salt. It has a special seafood flavor.

11 Sesame Oil (large bottle) is made by baking or steaming white or black sesame seeds and then extracting the oil. High quality sesame oil has a light color and strong fragrance.

Chili Oil (small bottle) is made by mixing a little water with chili powder then pouring it into hot vegetable oil and allowing it to cool. Ready-made chili oil is available in markets.

12 Barbecue (Sa Tsa) Sauce is made by grinding several different kinds of hot and fragrant spices and mixing them together. Ready-made Sa Tsa sauce is also available in markets.

13 Dried Seaweed should be rinsed and soaked in water for 10 minutes or until soft before using.

14 Dried Shaved Bonito is made by steaming, fermenting, drying, then shaving the bonito into thin slices. It is usually packed in a bag and is available in oriental food sections of supermarkets. Regular bonito (left side) may be used to cook soup. High quality bonito (right side) may be sprinkled on top of the dish and served.

15 Rice Noodles (left side) are a type of thin, dried thread made from rice starch.
Bean Threads (right side) are thin, dried bean threads made from mung beans. Soak the beans in water until they are soft before using them.

16 Chinese Black Mushrooms are an edible fungi that grow on dead tree trunks. Soak them in warm water until soft; cut off stem before using them.

Dried Wood Ears are an edible fungi that grow on dead tree trunks. The shape resembles a human ear. Soak wood ears in water until soft before using them. Large wood ears need to have the small hard stem removed before using.

Chicken Stock is made by adding water to chicken bones or chicken meat at the ratio of 4:1 then cooked one to two hours. Canned chicken stock is available in markets and is convenient to use.

Bread Crumbs are made by cutting off brown crust of white bread then left unwrapped to dry at room temperature for one to two hours. Tear bread into small pieces then grind them in a blender. For best results, grind a small amount of bread at a time. Ready-made bread crumbs are available in supermarkets.

調味醬汁做法
Preparing Seasoning Sauces

一道菜的成功與否，大半取決於調味是否適當，故本書除在內頁做菜部份介紹多種調味醬及沾汁外，特在此列出日常較常使用的調味醬、汁，以供讀者變化應用。下列調味醬除滷汁用於滷菜外，其他醬不僅可用來炒肉且可沾肉用。

Proper seasoning is the key to a tasteful dish. Besides the seasoning sauces and dipping sauces introduced in various recipes of this book, the following more popular sauces are listed for easy reference. Except for stewing sauce, all of the following sauces can be served as a dipping sauce.

1 乾燒醬 Spicy Ketchup Sauce pp. 62, 64, 70, 75

① 青葱白或洋葱（切碎）⋯ ⅓ 杯
　 蒜末、薑末⋯⋯⋯ 各 ½ 大匙
　 辣豆瓣醬或辣椒醬 1 小匙
② 番茄醬⋯⋯⋯⋯⋯ 3 大匙
　 酒、糖⋯⋯⋯⋯⋯ 各 1 大匙
　 鹽⋯⋯⋯⋯⋯⋯⋯ ½ 小匙
　 麻油、太白粉⋯⋯ 各 ½ 大匙
　 雞湯或水⋯⋯⋯⋯⋯ ¾ 杯

① ⅓ c. white part of green onions or onion, chopped
½ T. each: minced garlic, ginger root
1 t. hot bean paste or chili paste

② 3 T. ketchup, ½ t. salt
1 T. each: wine, sugar
½ T. each: sesame oil, cornstarch
¾ c. stock or water

2 豉汁醬 Black Bean Sauce pp. 49, 59, 64, 69, 79, 81

① 豆豉（剁碎）⋯⋯⋯ 3 大匙
　 蒜末⋯⋯⋯⋯⋯⋯ 1½ 大匙
　 葱、薑末⋯⋯⋯⋯⋯ 1 大匙
② 酒、太白粉⋯⋯ 各 1⅓ 大匙
　 醬油⋯⋯⋯⋯⋯⋯ 2 大匙
　 鹽⋯⋯⋯⋯⋯⋯⋯ ½ 小匙
　 糖、麻油⋯⋯⋯ 各 1 大匙
　 胡椒⋯⋯⋯⋯⋯⋯ ¼ 小匙
　 水⋯⋯⋯⋯⋯⋯⋯⋯ 1 杯

① 3 T. fermented black beans, minced
1½ T. minced garlic
1 T. each: minced green onions, ginger root

② 1⅓ T. each: wine, cornstarch
2 T. soy sauce, ½ t. salt
1 T. each: sugar, sesame oil
¼ t. pepper, 1 c. water

3 宮保醬 Hot Spicy Sauce pp. 34, 49, 64, 69, 83

① 乾辣椒⋯⋯⋯⋯⋯⋯ 2 支
　（切 1 公分長去籽）
　 蒜末⋯⋯⋯⋯⋯⋯⋯ 1 大匙
② 醬油、水⋯⋯⋯⋯ 各 ½ 杯
　 糖、酒⋯⋯⋯⋯⋯ 各 2 大匙
　 醋、太白粉⋯⋯ 各 1⅓ 大匙
　 麻油⋯⋯⋯⋯⋯⋯ ½ 大匙

① 2 dried hot peppers, cut into ½-inch long, remove seeds
1 T. minced garlic

② ½ c. each: soy sauce, water
2 T. each: sugar, wine
1⅓ T. each: vinegar, cornstarch
½ T. sesame oil

4 魚香醬 Spicy Hunan Sauce pp. 33, 59, 62, 64, 71, 77

① 辣豆瓣醬（或辣椒醬）1 大匙
　 葱、薑、蒜末⋯⋯ 各 1 大匙
② 醬油、水⋯⋯⋯⋯ 各 ½ 杯
　 糖、酒⋯⋯⋯⋯⋯ 各 2 大匙
　 醋、太白粉、麻油 1⅓ 大匙
　 花椒粉或胡椒⋯⋯⋯ ¼ 小匙

① 1 T. hot bean paste or chili paste
1 T. each: minced green onions, ginger root, garlic

② ½ c. each: soy sauce, water
2 T. each: sugar, wine
1⅓ T. each: vinegar, cornstarch, sesame oil
¼ t. peppercorn powder or pepper

1 2 3 4 醬的做法：油 2 大匙燒熱炒香①料隨入②料煮開即成約 1 杯醬。除乾燒醬可煮 6 兩肉（225 公克）外，其餘可煮約 1 斤肉（675 公克）。

1 2 3 4 Heat 2 T. oil. Stir-fry ① until fragrant. Mix and add ② ; cook until liquid thickens. Sauce **1** may be used for cooking ½ lb. (225g) meat while sauces **2**, **3** and **4** are for 1½ lb. (675g) meat.

5 家常烤醬 Home Style Baking Sauce

① 醬油⋯⋯⋯⋯⋯⋯ ¾ 杯
糖、酒⋯⋯⋯⋯⋯ 各 ¼ 杯
蒜末⋯⋯⋯⋯⋯⋯ 1½ 大匙
胡椒⋯⋯⋯⋯⋯⋯ ⅓ 小匙

① {
¾ c. soy sauce
¼ c. each: sugar, wine
1½ T. minced garlic
⅓ t. pepper
}

6 芝麻烤醬 Sesame Baking Sauce

① 海鮮醬或甜麵醬⋯⋯ 6 大匙
酒、醬油、糖⋯⋯ 各 4 大匙
蒜末、白芝麻⋯⋯ 各 1 大匙

① {
6 T. hoisin sauce or
sweet bean paste
4 T. each: wine, soy
sauce, sugar
1 T. each: minced garlic,
white sesame seeds
}

7 烤肉醬 Mongolian Barbecue Sauce

① 酒⋯⋯⋯⋯⋯⋯⋯ ⅓ 杯
醬油⋯⋯⋯⋯⋯⋯ ⅔ 杯
糖⋯⋯⋯⋯⋯⋯⋯ 3 大匙
太白粉⋯⋯⋯⋯⋯ ¾ 大匙

① {
⅓ c. wine
⅔ c. soy sauce
3 T. sugar
¾ T. cornstarch
}

8 滷汁 Stewing Sauce

① 深色醬油⋯⋯⋯⋯⋯ 1 杯
（如無可使用普通醬油）
普通醬油⋯⋯⋯⋯⋯ 1 杯
鹽⋯⋯⋯⋯⋯⋯⋯ 1½ 小匙
酒⋯⋯⋯⋯⋯⋯⋯ 6 大匙
冰糖或糖⋯⋯⋯⋯ 4 大匙
滷汁香料包⋯⋯⋯⋯ 1 包
或五香粉⋯⋯⋯ 1½ 小匙
或花椒 ½ 大匙、八角 2 朵

① {
1 c. dark soy sauce or
regular soy sauce
1 c. regular soy sauce
1½ t. salt, 6 T. wine
4 T. rock sugar or sugar
1 spice pouch, or
1½ t. five-spice powder,
or ½ T. szechuan
peppercorns and 2
star anises
}

9 鳳梨糖醋醬 Sweet & Sour Pineapple Sauce

① 新鮮鳳梨或罐裝⋯⋯⋯ 1 杯
（切小丁）
鳳梨汁、糖⋯⋯⋯ 各 ½ 杯
醋⋯⋯⋯⋯⋯⋯⋯ ⅓ 杯
鹽⋯⋯⋯⋯⋯⋯⋯ ¾ 小匙
太白粉⋯⋯⋯⋯⋯ 1 大匙

① {
1 c. fresh or canned
pineapple, diced
½ c. each: pineapple
juice, sugar
⅓ c. vinegar, ¾ t. salt
1 T. cornstarch
}

10 番茄糖醋醬 Sweet & Sour Ketchup

① 番茄醬、醋⋯⋯⋯ 各 ⅓ 杯
糖⋯⋯⋯⋯⋯⋯⋯ ½ 杯
鹽⋯⋯⋯⋯⋯⋯⋯ ¾ 小匙
水⋯⋯⋯⋯⋯⋯⋯ ½ 杯
太白粉⋯⋯⋯⋯⋯ 1 大匙

① {
⅓ c. each: ketchup,
vinegar
½ c. sugar
¾ t. salt
½ c. water
1 T. cornstarch
}

11 醬油糖醋醬 Sweet & Sour Soy Sauce

① 醬油、糖、醋⋯⋯ 各 ⅓ 杯
水⋯⋯⋯⋯⋯⋯⋯ 1 杯
太白粉⋯⋯⋯⋯⋯ 1 大匙
麻油⋯⋯⋯⋯⋯⋯ ½ 大匙

① {
⅓ c. each: soy sauce,
sugar, vinegar
1 c. water
1 T. cornstarch
½ T. sesame oil
}

12 檸檬糖醋醬 Sweet & Sour Lemon Sauce

① 新鮮檸檬切薄片⋯⋯ ½ 個
檸檬（擠汁）⋯⋯⋯ ⅓ 杯
糖⋯⋯⋯⋯⋯⋯⋯ ½ 杯
水⋯⋯⋯⋯⋯⋯⋯ 1 杯
鹽⋯⋯⋯⋯⋯⋯⋯ ¾ 小匙
太白粉⋯⋯⋯⋯⋯ 1 大匙

① {
½ fresh lemon, sliced
⅓ c. fresh lemon juice
½ c. sugar
1 c. water
¾ t. salt
1 T. cornstarch
}

13 酸梅糖醋醬 Sweet & Sour Plum Sauce

① 梅肉、糖⋯⋯⋯ 各 1½ 大匙
番茄醬⋯⋯⋯⋯⋯ 1 大匙
水⋯⋯⋯⋯⋯⋯⋯ 4 大匙
太白粉⋯⋯⋯⋯⋯ 1 小匙

① {
1½ T. each: sour plum,
sugar
1 T. ketchup
4 T. water
1 t. cornstarch
}

5 6 ①料拌勻，**7** 酒煮開後倒入①料煮 2 分鐘成濃汁，烤肉時任選烤醬拌入肉內，醃 ½ 小時以上，或邊烤邊塗，亦可沾食。1 杯醬可烤淨肉約 2 斤半（1350 公克）或帶骨約 4 斤（2250 公克），見 22、23、24 頁。

8 ①料燒開改小火煮 5 分鐘即成。滷肉時要加 3 倍的水使用，2 杯滷汁可滷約 3 斤肉（1800 公克），見 17 頁。

9 10 11 12 13 ①料煮開即可煮肉或沾食用，2 杯醬可煮約 1 斤肉（675 公克），見 44、45、46、47、74 頁。

5 6 Mix ① together. **7** Bring ⅓ cup wine to a boil. Add ① to wine and cook 2 minutes or until liquid thickens. To use any of the baking or barbecue sauces, marinate meat in sauce at least 30 minutes then bake, OR baste meat with sauce during baking. One cup of sauce may be used for baking 3 lbs. (1350g) boneless meat or 5 lbs. (2250g) meat with bone. See pp. 22, 23, 24 for uses of the sauces.

8 Bring ① to a boil; turn heat to low and cook 5 minutes to make sauce. Mix 1 portion of sauce to 3 portions of water when stewing meat. Two cups of sauce may be used for stewing 4 lbs. (1800g) meat. See p. 17 for uses of the sauce.

9 10 11 12 13 Bring ① to a boil to make sauces. Two cups of any sauce may be used for cooking 1½ lbs. (675g) meat. They may also be served as dipping sauce. See pp. 44, 45, 46, 47, 74 for uses of the sauces.

沙拉醬做法
Preparing Salad Sauces

  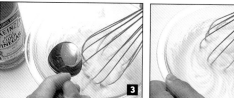 

Serves 4-6

① {
蛋黃 ·····················1 個
芥末粉或醬 ·············1 小匙
鹽、糖 ················各 1 小匙
}
沙拉油 ·····················¾ 杯
醋 ························1 大匙

① {
1 egg yolk
1 t. mustard powder or sauce
1 t. each: salt, sugar
}
¾ c. oil
1 T. vinegar

基本沙拉醬

①料盛入容器內（圖 1）開始時慢慢邊攪拌邊滴入油（圖 2），若一下放太多油會分離成稀糊狀。變硬時滴入少量醋使其變軟（圖 3）。如此反覆加油、加醋把全部材料加完（圖 4），即成一般「沙拉醬」。

Basic Salad Sauce

Put ① in a container (Fig. 1). Gradually add and stir oil into ① (Fig. 2); do not add too much oil at a time. If sauce becomes hard, add a little vinegar to soften it (Fig.3). Continue adding and stirring oil and vinegar to ① until they are mixed well (Fig. 4).

■ 芝麻沙拉醬
將芝麻醬（或花生醬）、醬油各 1 大匙，「基本沙拉醬」6 大匙，黑或白芝麻½ 大匙拌勻即成。

■ 芥末沙拉醬
芥末粉或醬半大匙置於容器內，徐徐拌入醬油 1 大匙及「基本沙拉醬」6 大匙即成。

■ 咖哩沙拉醬
咖哩粉½ 大匙置於容器內，徐徐拌入「基本沙拉醬」6 大匙，再加入洋蔥末½ 大匙，香菜末 1 小匙拌勻即成。

■ 茄汁沙拉醬
「基本沙拉醬」6 大匙拌入番茄醬 1½ 大匙、檸檬汁 1 小匙、洋蔥末 1 大匙、香菜末 1 小匙即成。

■ 鮮奶油沙拉醬
「基本沙拉醬」6 大匙徐徐拌入鮮奶油 2 大匙、檸檬汁 1 小匙即成。

■ 綜合沙拉醬
「基本沙拉醬」6 大匙徐徐拌入鮮奶油 1½ 大匙、番茄醬 1½ 大匙，最後加入青椒末、洋蔥末各半大匙，香菜末 1 小匙拌勻即成。

1 Sesame Salad Sauce
Mix together 1 T. each of sesame paste (or peanut butter) and soy sauce, 6 T. of basic salad sauce, and ½ T. of black or white sesame seeds.

2 Mustard Salad Sauce
Put ½ T. mustard powder or sauce in a container. Gradually add and stir 1 T. soy sauce and 6 T. basic salad sauce to mustard; stir until mixed well.

3 Curry Salad Sauce
Put ½ T. curry powder in a container. Gradually add and stir 6 T. basic salad sauce to curry powder. Mix ½ T. minced onion and 1 t. minced coriander into the sauce; stir until mixed well.

4 Ketchup Salad Sauce
Mix together 6 T. basic salad sauce, 1½ T. ketchup, 1 t. lemon juice, 1 T. minced onion, and 1 t. minced coriander.

5 Whipping Cream Salad Sauce
Gradually add 2 T. whipping cream and 1 t. lemon juice to 6 T. basic salad sauce; stir until mixed well.

6 Mixed Salad Sauce
Gradually add 1½ T. whipping cream and 1½ T. ketchup to 6 T. basic salad sauce. Add ½ T. each of minced green pepper and onion, 1 t. minced coriander to the sauce; stir until mixed well.

☐ The above shown sauces 1 - 6 serves 2-3.

☐ 1 ～ 6 醬均為 2-3 人份

沙拉汁做法
Preparing Salad Dressings

① {
鹽、糖…………各¾小匙
醋或檸檬汁………2大匙
黑胡椒…………⅙小匙
}
沙拉油…………6大匙

① {
³/₄ t. each: salt, sugar
2 T. vinegar or lemon juice
dash of black pepper
}
6 T. oil

基本沙拉汁
將①料拌入沙拉油即成。
醋採用蘋果醋或米醋味較佳。

Basic Salad Dressing
Add ① to 6 T. oil; stir until mixed well. Apple cider vinegar or rice vinegar may be substituted for vinegar for better flavor.

■1 蒜葱沙拉汁
「基本沙拉汁」½杯加入蒜粉1小匙、洋葱末3大匙拌勻即成。

■2 醬油沙拉汁
「基本沙拉汁」½杯加入醬油及青葱末各1大匙拌勻。

■3 梅肉沙拉汁
「基本沙拉汁」½杯加入漬梅肉壓碎剁爛1大匙拌勻。

■4 香芹沙拉汁
「基本沙拉汁」½杯加入香菜末1大匙、芹菜末2大匙拌勻。

■5 綜合沙拉汁
「基本沙拉汁」½杯加入去皮番茄切丁3大匙，熟鷄蛋切丁1個，青椒、洋葱、芹菜切碎各1大匙拌勻。

■6 蒜泥芥末沙拉汁
「基本沙拉汁」½杯加入蒜泥（用磨板磨成泥狀或剁爛成泥）½大匙、芥末¾小匙、洋葱末1½大匙拌勻。

■7 黃瓜沙拉汁
「基本沙拉汁」½杯加入小黃瓜1條（用磨板粗面磨碎）、芥末粉½小匙、洋葱末1小匙，拌勻即成。如無磨板，全部材料用果汁機攪碎亦可。

■8 蜂蜜沙拉汁
蜂蜜6大匙、醋2大匙、水2大匙、鹽⅙小匙拌勻。

■1 Garlic & Onion Salad Dressing
Add together 1 t. garlic powder and 3 T. minced onion to ¹/₂ cup basic salad dressing; stir until mixed well.

■2 Soy Sauce Salad Dressing
Add together 1 T. each of soy sauce and minced green onions to ¹/₂ cup of basic salad dressing; stir until mixed well.

■3 Plum Salad Dressing
Add together 1 T. mashed, salted sour plums to ¹/₂ cup basic salad dressing; stir until mixed well.

■4 Celery & Coriander Salad Dressing
Add together 1 T. minced coriander and 2 T. minced celery to ¹/₂ cup basic salad dressing; stir until mixed well.

■5 Mixed Salad Dressing
Add together 3 T. chopped and peeled tomato, one cooked and diced egg; 1 T. each of minced green pepper, onion, and celery to ¹/₂ cup of basic salad dressing; stir until mixed well.

■6 Mashed Garlic & Mustard Salad Dressing
Add together ¹/₂ T. mashed garlic, ³/₄ t. mustard, and 1¹/₂ T. minced onion to ¹/₂ cup basic salad dressing; stir until mixed well.

■7 Cucumber Salad Dressing
Grind one cucumber with a grinder. Add together cucumber, ¹/₂ t. mustard, and 1 t. minced onion to ¹/₂ cup of basic salad dressing; stir until mixed well. If a grinder is not available, use a blender.

■8 Honey Salad Dressing
Mix together 6 T. honey, 2 T. vinegar, 2 T. water and ¹/₆ t. salt; stir until mixed well.

鷄去骨取肉法
Boning Chicken

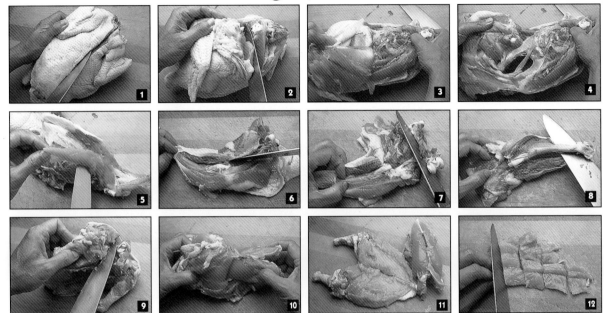

全鷄

1 鷄胸及背部各劃一刀,深觸及骨。

2 在鷄翅關節處下刀,切開關節,另一邊亦同。

3 抓住兩邊鷄翅,往下拉開至腿部。

4 抓住鷄腿往外拉開,關節處要切開;往下再拉使鷄肉與鷄骨全部分開。

5 胸骨兩側各切一刀觸骨,取出里肌肉。

鷄腿

6 鷄腿在內側大骨上面直切一刀,深觸及骨。

7 在上關節處切開剔去骨。

8 在下關節處切開剔去骨。

鷄胸

9 切開鷄翅與鷄胸關節連接處,另一邊亦同。

10 抓住兩邊鷄翅往下拉開。

11 取下鷄胸肉。

12 切鷄丁時可隨喜好去皮或連皮切丁。

Whole chicken

1 Make deep cuts on each side of breast and back; the cuts should reach bones.

2 Cut to separate joints of chicken wings.

3 Hold wings and pull down to legs.

4 Pull legs to the sides; cut to separate joints. Separate meat from bones by pulling down on the legs.

5 Make a cut on each side of breast bone; cuts should reach the bone. Remove breast meat.

Chicken leg

6 Make a deep cut to the bone on inside surface of chicken leg.

7 Cut on upper joint of the leg to remove bone.

8 Cut on lower joint of the leg to remove bone.

Chicken breast

9 Cut through joints between the chicken wings and breast.

10 Hold both chicken wings and pull down.

11 Remove breast meat.

12 Chicken meat may be diced with or without skin.

全雞切塊分解動作
Cutting Whole Chicken

一隻雞可分切成雞背、雞胸、雞腿、雞翅等 6 大塊。
A whole chicken can be cut into six parts: back, breast, legs, and wings.

 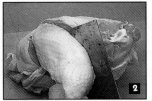  

1 切開雞翅關節取下雞翅，另一邊亦同。

2 沿雞腿兩側劃兩刀，深觸及骨。

3 往上拉開取下雞腿。

4 從腹部橫剖開，取下雞胸。

1 Cut through joints of the chicken wings to remove the wings.

2 Make two deep cuts along both sides of the legs, cuts should reach the bones.

3 Pull up on the legs to remove them.

4 Make a horizontal cut on the belly of the chicken to remove breast.

醃肉要領及炒法
Tips for Marinating and Stir-frying

1 肉調入醃料，攪拌至醃汁完全被吸收有黏性；再加太白粉拌勻，炒前拌入油容易散開。

2 鍋（可使用中國炒鍋、平底鍋或不黏鍋等）先燒熱再放 1½ 大匙油，隨即輕搖鍋子，使油均佈鍋面。

3 4 5 隨入肉丁、肉片或肉絲，散開於鍋面煎約 15 秒。

6 煎至金黃色；翻面炒開至七分熟，鏟於鍋邊。

7 餘油略炒配料（任選喜好蔬菜），加入調味汁、肉等蓋鍋，見水蒸氣冒出，全部材料拌炒均勻即成。

可將多量肉切好拌入醃料，分裝冷凍保存。每次取一份解凍加太白粉拌勻，炒前加油 1 大匙使用。
Large quantities of meat may be cut, marinated, and stored in several small bags then frozen for later use. Defrost one bag of meat for each use; mix meat with cornstarch. Combine with 1 T. oil before frying.

1 Add marinade to the meat and stir until it is absorbed and becomes sticky, then add cornstarch. To separate meat during stir-frying, add oil to the marinated meat before frying.

2 Heat a pan (Chinese wok, frying pan, or non-stick pan, etc. may be used) then add 1½ T. oil; swirl the oil in the pan to spread the oil evenly.

3 4 5 Separate the pieces of meat in pan then fry 15 seconds.

6 Fry the meat until it is golden brown; turn it over and stir-fry until medium well. Remove meat from pan or move it to the side.

7 Use the remaining oil to lightly stir-fry the trimmings. Add sauce and meat; cover and cook until steaming then stir to combine.

牛、豬肉種類及用途
Beef and Pork Used in Recipes in This Book

1 紐約牛排　是最好的牛排肉，較瘦，故煎過熟肉質會變硬。

2 菱眼牛排　形狀像眼睛而名之，肉質很嫩，但夾層油質較多。

3 丁型骨牛排　中含 T 型骨頭，食用時較不方便，但肉質很好。

4 腰肉牛排　一般中國餐館或家庭切片或切絲，當高級炒牛肉用。

5 菲力牛排小里肌　牛小里肌肉肉質很嫩，煎、烤都適宜。

6 牛大排骨　適合煮湯或燒烤使用。

1 **New York Steak** is the best steak because it is lean. However it will become hard if overcooked.

2 **Rib Eye Steak** is tender but has fat marbled through it.

3 **T-bone Steak** is a good quality meat.

4 **Flank Steak** is usually sliced or shredded and used as high quality stir-fried beef in Chinese restaurants and for Chinese home cooking.

5 **Filet mignon steak** is tender and suitable for frying or roasting.

6 **Beef Back Ribs** are suitable for cooking stock or barbecue.

7 牛小排骨片 牛小排骨鋸成薄片，煎、烤、炸、煮均可。

8 牛尾 煮湯或紅燒用。

9 牛腱 即牛小腿肉，適合於紅燒。牛腩、肋條用法同。

10 豬大小里肌 是豬肉最嫩的部份，煎、炒兩相宜。

11 豬大排 煎或烤用。

12 豬小排 炸、烤或煮湯均可。

13 牛、豬絞肉 使用範圍廣，煎、炒、炸、煮均可。

7 **Beef Flank Ribs** may be sliced and used for frying, roasting, deep-frying, and cooking in sauces.

8 **Beef Oxtails** are suitable for cooking soups or cooking in sauces.

9 **Beef Shank** is the meat from the leg of the beef and is suitable to cook in sauces.

10 **Pork Loin and Tenderloin** are the most tender parts of pork meat and are suitable for frying or stir-frying.

11 **Pork Loin Center Cuts** are suitable for frying or roasting.

12 **Pork Back Ribs** are suitable for deep-frying, roasting or cooking soups.

13 **Ground beef and pork** are widely used and are suitable for frying, stir-frying, deep-frying and steaming.

蝦仁處理及炒法
Preparing and Stir-frying Shrimp

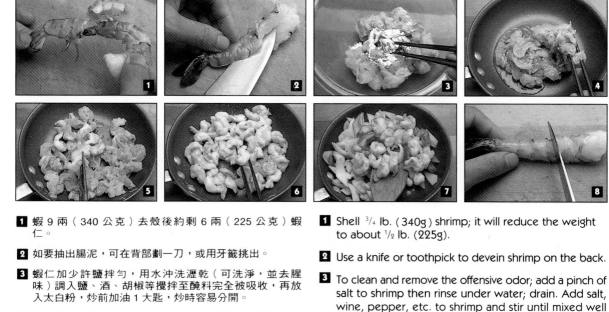

1. 蝦 9 兩（340 公克）去殼後約剩 6 兩（225 公克）蝦仁。

2. 如要抽出腸泥，可在背部劃一刀，或用牙籤挑出。

3. 蝦仁加少許鹽拌勻，用水沖洗瀝乾（可洗淨，並去腥味）調入鹽、酒、胡椒等攪拌至醃料完全被吸收，再放入太白粉，炒前加油 1 大匙，炒時容易分開。

4. 鍋燒熱，用油 1½ 大匙，將鍋輕搖，使油均勻遍佈於鍋面，放入蝦仁。

5. 煎約 15 秒後翻面再煎。

6. 煎至七分熟，顏色成淡紅色，蝦肉略收縮時鏟開。

7. 鍋內炒配料及調味汁，蓋鍋見水蒸氣冒出拌炒均勻即成。

8. 若炸蝦，則炸前先在腹部切三刀，深至一半，炸時才不會捲縮。

蝦新鮮的可一次多買，去殼調味後分裝冷凍，每次取一份解凍，加太白粉拌勻，炒前加油 1 大匙使用。

1. Shell ³/₄ lb. (340g) shrimp; it will reduce the weight to about ¹/₂ lb. (225g).

2. Use a knife or toothpick to devein shrimp on the back.

3. To clean and remove the offensive odor; add a pinch of salt to shrimp then rinse under water; drain. Add salt, wine, pepper, etc. to shrimp and stir until mixed well then add cornstarch. Add 1 T. oil to shrimp before frying to prevent sticking together during frying.

4. Heat pan then add 1¹/₂ T. oil. Rotate pan to spread oil evenly then put in shrimp.

5. Fry shrimp about 15 seconds then turn over.

6. Continue to fry shrimp until medium well and color turns red; move shrimp to side of pan.

7. Stir-fry trimmings and sauce; cover and cook until steaming. Mix in shrimp and stir to combine.

8. For deep-frying shrimp, make three cuts to half way into belly of shrimp so it will not curl and shrink during frying.

If 5 lbs. (2250g) package of frozen shrimp is purchased (typical package), shell and marinate shrimp then divide and store in several small bags in freezer. Defrost one bag of shrimp for each use; mix shrimp with cornstarch. Combine with 1 T. oil before frying.

魚去骨取肉法
Preparing and Filleting Fish

  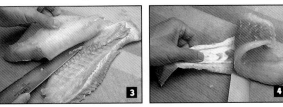

1. 用刮鱗器或刀將魚鱗刮除並洗淨，切開魚腹至鰓部，並取出鰓及內臟後洗淨。
2. 取肉時，先將頭部切除，再由背部劃一刀。
3. 沿着中間大骨片出魚肉，同法片出另一邊魚肉。
4. 去魚皮時，由尾端切深至魚皮處，再斜刀往前切開取下魚皮，即為魚排淨肉。

1. Scale fish then rinse. Cut along belly to gills. Remove and discard gills and entrails.
2. Cut off head before filleting. Cut from the back of fish.
3. Cut by sliding blade along backbone and over ribs to release flesh in one piece. Use the same procedure to release flesh from the other side.
4. To skin fish, slant knife from tail end and push knife forward to remove skin. The flesh will be removed easily.

蟹處理法
Preparing Crab

1. 打開蟹蓋，除去鰓，洗淨。
2. 剁開蟹鉗及蟹腳。
3. 蟹鉗切半或搥破。
4. 蟹身順著腳的方向切成 6 小塊。

1. Open shell and remove the crab gills then rinse.
2. Cut off legs and claws.
3. Cut claws in half or crack them with a mallet.
4. Cut body of crab into 6 pieces.

魷魚、墨魚處理法
Preparing Squid and Cuttlefish

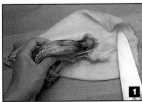  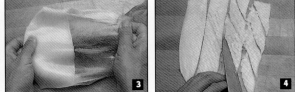

1. 將魷魚身切開，取出內臟，切開頭部。
2. 魷魚身頭部劃一刀至表皮。
3. 撕除外面薄皮。
4. 在內面斜劃交叉刀痕深至 $\frac{2}{3}$ 處，直切四條，再切菱形塊。

1. Cut squid to open the body. Discard all material from body. Cut off head.
2. Make a cut at the head end of hood.
3. Peel off membrane from hood.
4. Make diagonal cuts to $2/3$ deep on inside surface. Turn squid and make diagonal cuts from opposite direction to $2/3$ deep to form diamond-shape cuts, cut hood into four strips then cut them into rhomboid-shaped pieces.

三味白切雞
Flavored Boiled Chicken

① 雞 1 隻 …… 約 2 斤（1350公克）
酒 ……………………………… 3 大匙
鹽 ……………………………… 1 大匙
青葱（切7.5公分長段）…… 1 枝
薑（切片）…………………… 2 片
沾汁 ……………………………… 適量

① 1 chicken, 3 lbs. (1350g)
3 T. wine
1 T. salt
1 green onion, cut to 3-inch long
2 slices of ginger root

DIPPING SAUCE

1 ①料調勻塗抹雞身內外醃半小時以上。

2 將雞放入滾水內（水淹過雞身）大火煮開後去除上面泡沫改小火蓋鍋煮 30 分鐘至熟取出待涼，切塊沾「沾汁」或將沾汁澆淋在雞肉上，可以蔬菜圍邊。

☐ 用微波爐需 12-15 分鐘。用蒸鍋需水開大火，雞胸朝上蒸 25 分鐘。

沾汁（任選一）
A 醬油 4 大匙、麻油 $\frac{1}{2}$ 大匙拌勻。

B 醬油 4 大匙，糖、醋、麻油各 $\frac{1}{2}$ 大匙，蒜泥 1 大匙，辣油 $\frac{1}{2}$ 大匙或辣椒醬 1 小匙拌勻。亦可酌加花生醬。

1 Mix and rub ① on skin and inside chicken; marinate at least 30 minutes.

2 Place chicken in boiling water; water should cover chicken. Boil again; remove foam and scum. Turn heat to low; cover and cook 30 minutes. Remove chicken and let cool. To serve, cut chicken into pieces then dip in dipping sauce or sprinkle sauce over chicken. Sliced vegetables may be arranged around plate as garnish.

☐ Microwave use; set at high for 12 to 15 minutes. For steamer; bring water to boil, steam chicken, breast up, for 25 minutes.

DIPPING SAUCES (choose one of the following):
A Mix 4 T. soy sauce with $\frac{1}{2}$ T. sesame oil.

B Mix together 4 T. soy sauce, $\frac{1}{2}$ T. each of sugar and vinegar, 1 T. mashed garlic, $\frac{1}{2}$ T. chili oil (or 1 t. chili paste), and $\frac{1}{2}$ T. sesame oil. Peanut butter may be added as desired.

滷鴨
Stewed Duck

鴨或雞 1 隻　3 斤半（2100公克）
（切成二半）

① 滷汁（見6頁）…………2½杯
　　水…………………………7 杯
　　黃豆………………………1 杯
　　麻油…………………………少許

1　duck or chicken(cut in
　　half), 4-5 lbs.(2100g)
① 2½ c. stewing sauce
　　　(see p. 6)
　　7　c. water
　　1　c. soybeans
　sesame oil as desired

■ 鴨及①料大火煮開後蓋鍋，改小火煮30分鐘（中途翻面），熄火續浸約15分
　鐘後取出。待涼塗上少許麻油剁塊，淋上滷汁。如滷雞腿僅需煮15分鐘。

滷黃豆 黃豆泡水10小時後，瀝乾水份，加入滷鴨汁1½杯，中火煮25分鐘。

■ Bring ① and duck to boil; cover and reduce heat to low and cook
　30 minutes (turn duck during cooking). Turn off heat and allow duck
　to soak about 15 minutes. Remove duck and let cool. Reserve sauce.
　Rub sesame oil over duck and cut in pieces. Sprinkle stewing sauce
　over duck; serve. If chicken legs are used , stew only 15 minutes.

STEWED SOYBEANS Soak soybeans in water for 10 hours; drain and
cook over medium heat in 1½ cups liquid reserved from stewing duck
for 25 minutes.

烤全雞
Roast Chicken

雞 1 隻 ……　約 2 斤（1350公克）

① 鹽…………………………½大匙
　　五香粉或胡椒…………¼小匙
　　蜂蜜……………………3 大匙

1　chicken, 3 lbs. (1350g)
　　½ T. salt
① ¼ t. five-spice powder or
　　　pepper
　　3　T. honey

■ 多量熱水冲泡雞約 5 分鐘後拭乾，趁熱將蜂蜜塗在雞皮上，①料放入肚
　內抹勻，用 350°～375°F 烤 50 分鐘即成。可與生菜沙拉（見 92-95 頁）
　共食。

■ Rinse chicken with hot water about 5 minutes then pat dry. Rub honey
　on skin while chicken is hot. Rub ① evenly inside chicken then roast at
　350°F -375°F about 50 minutes. Serve with vegetable salad (see pp.
　92-95) if desired.

塡飯雞
Chicken Stuffed with Rice

雞或鴨 1 隻 ……………… 約 2 斤
　　　　　　　　　　（1350 公克）
① { 酒……2 大匙、鹽……½ 大匙
　　胡椒………………………… 少許
　　紅葱頭或葱片………… 2 大匙
② { 紅蘿蔔丁、筍丁　}
　　香菇丁、青豆仁　} …… 共 1 杯
　　（或冷凍綜合蔬菜）
③ { 米（任何米種）…………¾ 杯
　　水…………………… 1¼ 杯
④ { 醬油…1½ 大匙、糖… 1 小匙
　　胡椒、麻油………………… 少許
　　牙籤或鐵籤……………… 適量
　　醬油…………………… 2 大匙
⑤ { 蠔油或醬油………… 2 大匙
　　糖…1 小匙、太白粉…1½ 大匙
　　雞湯或水………………… 2 杯
　　葱花…………………… 2 大匙

1 chicken or duck, 3 lbs.
   (1350g)
① { 2 T. wine, ½ T. salt
   dash of pepper
   2 T. sliced green onions or
      shallots
② { total of 1 c.: green peas,
      diced Chinese black
      mushrooms (softened in
      water), bamboo shoots,
      carrot
   or 1 c. frozen mixed
      vegetables
③ { ³/₄ c. rice
   1¹/₄ c. water
④ { 1¹/₂ T. soy sauce, 1 t. sugar
   dash of pepper
   sesame oil as desired
   toothpicks or skewers
   2 T. soy sauce
⑤ { 2 T. oyster sauce or soy
      sauce
   2 c. chicken stock or water
   1 t. sugar, 1¹/₂ T. cornstarch
   2 T. chopped green onions

1 用①料抹勻雞身內外。米洗淨泡 1 小時。

2 油 2 大匙先炒香葱，隨入②料略炒後加③、④料翻炒約 5 分鐘至汁收乾。趁熱塡入雞肚內，用牙籤封口，以 375°F 烤 90 分鐘（中途翻面）。

3 將⑤料煮開成濃稠狀，淋在雞肉上，撒上葱花。

塡飯火雞 火雞較雞大 2-3 倍，②、③、④塡雞料增爲 2 倍，烤的時間延長爲 3-4 小時。

1 Rub cavity and skin of chicken with ① ; marinate. Rinse rice then soak in water 1 hour.

2 Heat 2 T. oil then stir-fry onions until fragrant. Add ② and stir briefly. Add ③ and ④ ; stir-fry 5 minutes or until liquid is almost evaporated. Stuff chicken with the hot mixture. Sew up opening with toothpicks. Roast chicken at 375°F 90 minutes; turn over during roasting.

3 Mix and bring ⑤ to boil and cook until thick. Pour sauce over chicken and sprinkle with chopped green onions.

TURKEY STUFFED WITH RICE Turkey is usually two or three times larger than chicken. Use twice the amount of stuffed ingredients and roast turkey 3 to 4 hours.

叫化鷄
Foiled Chicken

鷄 1 隻 ···· 約 2 斤（1350 公克）
乾荷葉或牛皮紙、鋁紙各 1 張

① { 酒 ······ 3 大匙、鹽 ······ 1 大匙
　　葱、薑 ······················· 少許

② { 香菇、豆干
　　筍、紅蘿蔔 } 切絲 ····· 共 2½ 杯

③ { 醬油 ··· 2½ 大匙、糖 ···· 1 小匙
　　胡椒 ·························· 少許

牙籤或線 ···················· 適量

1 chicken, 3 lbs. (1350g)
1 sheet each: lotus leaf or
　kraft paper bag,
　aluminum foil

① { 3 T. wine, 1 T. salt
　　green onions
　　ginger root as desired

② { total of 2½ c. (shredded):
　　bamboo shoots, Chinese
　　black mushrooms, carrot,
　　pressed bean curd

③ { 2½ T. soy sauce
　　1 t. sugar, dash of pepper

toothpicks or thread

1 乾荷葉（圖 1）泡熱水至軟，拭乾抹麻油。①料抹勻鷄身內外醃半小時。

2 麻油 1½ 大匙燒熱，炒香②料加③料炒勻後，填入鷄肚，以牙籤縫合開口，依序包上荷葉及鋁紙，用 400°F 烤 80 分鐘（中途翻面）。

☐ 可用西芹、洋菇、洋葱或其他蔬菜取代②料。

1 Soak dried lotus leaf (Fig. 1) in hot water until soft. Wipe dry and spread sesame oil over leaf. Rub cavity and skin of chicken with ① ; marinate 30 minutes.

2 Heat 1½ T. sesame oil. Stir-fry ② until fragrant. Add ③ and stir-fry until mixed well. Stuff chicken with mixture and sew up opening. Wrap chicken with lotus leaf then with aluminum foil. Roast at 400°F 80 minutes, turn over during baking.

☐ Celery, mushrooms, onion, or other vegetables may be substituted for ②.

家常鹽水鴨
Salty Duck

鴨 1 隻 ····· 3 斤半（2100 公克）

① { 酒 ······ 4 大匙、鹽 ······ 3 大匙
　　花椒粒 ·· 2 大匙、胡椒 ·· ¼ 小匙

② { 鹽 ··· 1 小匙、花椒粒 ·· ½ 大匙
　　葱 ······· 2 支、薑 ········· 4 片
　　酒 ······· 4 大匙、水 ······ 15 杯

麻油 ······················· 1 大匙

1 duck, 4-5 lbs.(1800-2250g)

① { 4 T. wine, 3 T. salt
　　2 T. Szechuan peppercorn
　　¼ t. pepper

② { 1 t. salt, 15 c. water
　　½ T. Szechuan peppercorn
　　2 green onions, 4 T. wine
　　4 slices of ginger root

1 T. sesame oil

1 用①料抹勻鴨身內外，醃半日或隔夜。煮時沖淨。

2 鴨放入②料，大火燒開後改小火蓋鍋煮 40 分鐘取出待冷，抹上麻油，冷藏可保存數天。食用時切塊。

☐ 鴨湯去除油漬留做高湯用，如用微波爐需 15～20 分鐘。

1 Rub cavity and skin of duck with ① ; marinate half a day or over night. Rinse before cooking.

2 Cook ② and duck; bring to boil. Reduce heat to low; cover and cook 40 minutes or until duck is cooked. Remove duck, let cool then spread with sesame oil. The duck may be kept fresh for several days if refrigerated; cut into pieces when ready to serve.

☐ Liquid left from cooking duck may be saved and used as stock after removing fat off the top. The duck may also be cooked in a microwave at high 15-20 minutes.

家常式北京烤鴨
Home Style Peiking Duck

鴨 1 隻 ····· 3 斤半(2100 公克)
蜂蜜·····························4 大匙

①
甜麵醬或海鮮醬··········3 大匙
水································¼ 杯
糖·····························3 大匙
麻油···························1 大匙

葱（切絲）··················½ 杯
荷葉餅或割包□··········12 張

1 duck, 4-5 lbs.
  (1800-2250g)
4 T. honey

①
3 T. sweet bean paste or
  Hoisin sauce
3 T. sugar
¼ c. water
1 T. sesame oil

12 mandarin pancakes or
  Taiwanese steamed
  turnovers□
½ c. shredded green onions

1 用多量熱水冲泡鴨約 5 分鐘，拭乾水份，趁熱用蜂蜜塗勻鴨皮表面，掛於通風處風乾，約 3～6 小時。皮越乾，烤出的鴨皮越脆，顏色亦佳。

2 鴨背朝上置烤架上，在烤箱中層用 350°F ～ 400°F 烤 1 小時（中途翻面），呈金黃色，肉熟即成。

3 ①料煮成濃稠狀後塗在餅上，包捲葱絲及鴨皮或肉食用。

□ 荷葉餅、割包做法參考「點心專輯」21 頁及 9 頁或買冷凍現成。

1 Use ample hot water to rinse and soak duck about 5 minutes; wipe dry. Rub honey over skin of duck then hang in a ventilated place to dry for 3 to 6 hours. Crispiness and color is determined by dryness. The drier the skin, the crispier and better color it will be after baking.

2 Put duck on rack, back side up, then place on middle shelf of oven. Roast at 350°F- 400 °F 1 hour or until cooked and golden, turn over during roasting.

3 Cook ① until thick then spread on a pancake; put in one portion of green onions and meat then roll up pancake. Follow same procedures for the other 11 portions. Serve.

□ Mandarin pancakes or Taiwanese Steamed turnovers, see pp. 21, 9 of *CHINESE SNACKS*. Frozen ready-made pancakes and turnovers are available in supermarkets.

廣東烤鴨
Cantonese Roast Duck

鴨 1 隻 ····· 3 斤半(2100 公克)

① 酒 ······· 2 大匙、鹽 ······· 1 大匙
　　葱 ················· 1 支 ⎫ 拍扁
　　薑 ················· 2 片 ⎭

五香粉或胡椒 ··········· ⅓ 小匙

牙籤 ····· 4 支、蜂蜜 ····· 4 大匙

沾汁：海鮮醬或酸梅醬（圖 1）

1　duck, 4-5 lbs.
　　(1800-2250g)

① 2　T. wine, 1 T. salt
　 1　green onion, pat flat
　 2　slices ginger root, pat flat

⅓　t. five-spice powder or
　　pepper

4　toothpicks

4　T. honey

DIPPING SAUCE: Hoisin
　　sauce or sweet & sour
　　plum sauce (Fig. 1)

1 ①料塗抹鴨身內外，醃半小時以上。用過的葱薑加五香粉抹勻鴨肚內，以牙籤封口備用。

2 參考左頁做法 **1**、**2** 在鴨上淋滾水及抹蜂蜜，掛於通風處 1 小時以上，烤熟切塊沾「沾汁」食之。

□ 海鮮醬、酸梅醬見 7 頁。

1 Rub ① in cavity and on skin of duck; marinate at least 30 minutes. Spread onions, ginger root of ① and five-spice powder in cavity of duck and seal opening with toothpicks.

2 Follow steps **1** and **2** on p. 20, except hang duck in a ventilated place at least 1 hour instead of 3 to 6 hours. Cut roasted duck in pieces; serve with dipping sauce. To make sour plum sauce, see p. 7.

燻鴨
Smoked Duck

鴨 1 隻 ····· 3 斤半(2100 公克)

① 料同上

② 茶葉 ··················· ½ 杯
　 糖 ···················· 4 大匙

沾汁：同上或

　　醬油 ················· 4 大匙
　　嫩薑絲、香菜末 ······· 各 2 大匙

1　duck, 4-5 lbs.
　　(1800-2250g)

① see ① in above recipe

② ½ c. tea leaves
　 4　T. sugar

DIPPING SAUCE: see dipping
　　sauce in above recipe or

4　T. soy sauce

2　T. each: baby ginger root,
　　minced fresh coriander

1 ①料塗抹鴨身內外，醃半小時以上。

2 烤盤內拌入②料，置於烤箱下層，鴨放在上層用 400℉ 燻烤 1 小時（烤時會冒烟），切塊沾「沾汁」。鴨亦可用水煮熟約 40 分鐘，再燻烤 25 分鐘即成。

1 Follow step **1** in above recipe and marinate duck at least 30 minutes.

2 Mix ② in baking pan and put pan on lower rack of oven. Place duck on top rack and roast at 400°F 1 hour (It will smoke during baking). Cut duck in pieces and serve with dipping sauce. OR boil duck 40 minutes then roast and smoke 25 minutes.

蜜汁鷄腿（2種口味）
Baked Flavored Chicken Legs

鷄腿肉 2 片 ····8 兩(300 公克)
蜂蜜·····················1 大匙
檸檬·····················2 片
沾汁 ·····················適量

2 slices of boneless chicken
  legs, ⅔ lb. (300g)
1 T. honey
2 slices lemon
DIPPING SAUCE

■ 備烤盤，鷄皮朝上，表面抹勻蜂蜜，用 375°F 烤 25-30 分鐘至表面呈金
黃色，皮脆肉熟即可。食用時洒上檸檬汁，再隨自己喜好沾「沾汁」。可
與蔬菜（見 88-95 頁）共食。

沾汁（任選一）：
🅰 烤肉醬（見 7 頁）。

🅱 醬油、檸檬汁各 2 大匙，醋 ½ 大匙拌勻。

■ Put meat, skin side up, in a baking pan then spread on honey. Bake at
375°F 25-30 minutes or until cooked and skin is golden brown and
crispy. Sprinkle lemon juice over meat and serve with desired dipping
sauce and vegetable (see pp. 88-95).

DIPPING SAUCES:
🅰 Mongolian barbecue sauce (see p. 7).

🅱 2 T. each of soy sauce & lemon juice, and ½ T. vinegar. Mix well.

家常鷄腿
Home Style Chicken Legs

鷄腿肉2片 ⋯⋯ 8 兩（300 公克）
① 醬油 ⋯⋯⋯⋯⋯⋯⋯⋯⋯ 3 大匙
　 糖、酒 ⋯⋯⋯⋯⋯ 各 1¼ 大匙
　 檸檬片 ⋯⋯⋯⋯⋯⋯⋯⋯⋯ 2 片

- 2 slices of boneless chicken legs, ²/₃ lb. (300g)
- ① { 3 T. soy sauce
　　 1¼ T. each: sugar, wine
- 2 slices of lemon

1 鷄腿肉調入①料，醃½小時以上或隔夜。

2 鷄肉置烤盤內，用 450°F 烤 25-30 分鐘，至表面呈深金黃色，灑上檸檬汁食用。

☐ 可隨喜好酌加蒜及辣椒於①料內。

☐ 家常烤醬（見 7 頁）5 大匙可取代①料。

1 Marinate meat in ① at least 30 minutes or over night.

2 Put meat in baking pan and bake at 450°F 25-30 minutes or until cooked and skin is golden brown. Sprinkle on lemon juice and serve.

☐ Garlic and hot chili pepper may be added to ① as desired.

☐ Substitute 5 T. home style baking sauce (see p. 7) for ingredients ① .

烤咖哩鷄腿
Baked Curry Chicken Legs

鷄腿肉 2 片 ⋯⋯ 8 兩（300 公克）
或鷄翅 ⋯⋯⋯ 12 兩（450 公克）
　 咖哩粉（圖 1）⋯⋯⋯⋯ 1 大匙
① 鹽 ⋯⋯ ½ 小匙、酒 ⋯⋯ 1 大匙
　 胡椒 ⋯⋯⋯⋯⋯⋯⋯⋯⋯ 少許

- 2 boneless chicken legs, ²/₃ lb. (300g) or 1 lb. (450g) chicken wings
- ① { 1 T. wine
　　 1 T. curry powder (Fig. 1)
　　 ½ t. salt
　　 dash of pepper

■ 鷄肉與①料拌勻，鷄皮朝上置烤盤內，用 450°F～500°F，烤 25～30 分鐘，至表面呈金黃色，皮脆肉熟即成。

■ Add ① to chicken legs; mix well. Put meat in baking pan, skin side up, then bake at 450°F-500°F 25-30 minutes or until cooked and skin is golden brown and crispy; remove.

1

各種串燒
Flavored Kabob

鶏肉（去皮）
蝦仁
牛肉
鮮貝
}　任選 9 兩
（340 公克）

洋葱
青葱
白葱
鮮菇類
青紅椒
紅蘿蔔或筍
}　任選適量

竹籤或鐵籤（12 公分）8 支

¾ lb. (340g) of the following as desired: skinless chicken, shelled shrimps, beef, scallops

desired amount of the following: onion, green onions, fresh mushrooms, green or red peppers, carrot or bamboo shoots

8 skewers or wooden sticks, 5-inch long

■ 材料全部切塊，用竹籤串成 8 串（圖 1）後，任選調味。

椒鹽味 撒上少許鹽、胡椒粉或花椒粉，

家常味 邊烤邊塗家常烤醬（見 7 頁）在串燒材料上（約 3 次），

咖哩味 撒上少許鹽及咖哩粉，

沙茶味 撒上少許鹽，抹上沙茶醬約 2 大匙，

在炭火上燒烤，並時時翻轉，約烤 10 分鐘至肉熟呈金黃色，或用烤箱 450°F-500°F 烤約 12-15 分鐘至表面呈金黃色肉熟即成。

醬味 串燒肉烤熟後表面塗上烤肉醬（見 7 頁）即成。

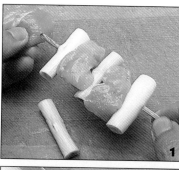

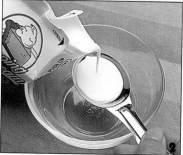

■ Cut all ingredients into small pieces then thread them equally on each skewer (Fig. 1).

PEPPERCORN SALT Sprinkle kabob with salt and pepper (or peppercorn).

HOME STYLE Brush kabob with home style baking sauce (see p. 7) about three times during barbecuing.

CURRY-FLAVORED Sprinkle kabob with dash of salt and curry powder.

SA TSA Sprinkle kabob with a dash of salt then spread 2 T. Sa Tsa sauce.

Barbecue the flavored kabob over charcoal until cooked; turn constantly during barbecuing.

MONGOLIAN BARBECUE Spread unflavored kabob with Mongolian barbecue sauce (see p. 7) after barbecuing.

咖哩鷄腿
Chicken Legs & Curry Sauce

鷄腿 2 隻 ···· 1 斤（ 600 公克 ）
奶油或沙拉油··············4 大匙
洋葱（ 切碎 ）···············½ 個
① ┤ 麵粉···· 4 大匙、蒜末··· 1 小匙
　　咖哩粉···············2½ 大匙
② ┤ 酒······ 2 大匙、水 ··· 2½ 杯
　　鹽······· 1⅓ 小匙、糖···2 小匙
　　胡椒··················少許
③　洋芋、紅蘿蔔（ 切塊 ）·····3 杯

2　chicken legs, 1⅓ lbs. (600g)
4　T. butter or oil
½　onion, chopped
① ┤ 4　T. flour
　　2½ T. curry powder
　　1　t. minced garlic
② ┤ 2　T. wine, 2½ c. water
　　1 ⅓ t. salt, 2 t. sugar
　　dash of pepper
③ ┤ 1　potato, 1　carrot,
　　　 cut into small pieces

1 將油燒熱小火炒香洋葱（ 約 4～5 分鐘呈金黃色 ），隨入①料略炒 1 分鐘，取出備用。可照比率多做儲存。

2 鷄腿在內側直劃深刀，與②、③料一起煮開後，改中火蓋鍋再煮 20 分鐘；用炒過①料勾芡成濃稠狀。

1 Heat oil and stir-fry onion over low heat until fragrant (4-5 minutes) then add ① and stir-fry 1 minute; remove. More may be made by increasing amount of ingredients at the same ratio. Unused portion may be stored for later use.

2 Make several vertical cuts on chicken legs. Cook chicken, ② , ③ ; bring to boil. Reduce heat to medium; cover and cook 20 minutes. Add the fried ① to thicken.

奶汁鷄腿
Chicken Legs & Milk

鷄腿 2 隻 ···· 1 斤（ 600 公克 ）
① ┤ 奶油或沙拉油··············2 大匙
　　洋葱(切碎) ¼ 個、蒜末 ½ 大匙
② 　水······· 1½ 杯，其他同上②料
③ ┤ 白花菜、洋菇
　　洋葱、紅蘿蔔 }··· 切塊共 3 杯
　　鮮奶油（圖 2）或濃縮奶水⅓ 杯
④ 　太白粉··· 3 大匙，　水··· 5 大匙

2　chicken legs, 1⅓ lbs. (600g)
① ┤ 2　T. oil or butter
　　¼　onion, chopped
　　½　T. minced garlic
② ┤ 1½ c. water
　　others see ② in above recipe
③ ┤ Total of 3 c. (cut into pieces):
　　　 cauliflower, mushrooms,
　　　 carrot, onion
　　⅓ c. whipping cream or
　　　 evaporated milk (Fig. 2)
④　3　T. cornstarch, 5 T. water

■ 將①料炒香，隨入②料及鷄腿（ 在內側直劃深刀 ），蓋鍋大火燒開後改中火煮 15 分鐘，再入③料續煮 5 分鐘，最後倒入奶水，用④料勾芡成濃稠狀。可與飯或麵共食。

□ 如無鮮奶油或濃縮奶水，可用鮮奶取代。

■ Make several vertical cuts on chicken. Stir-fry ① until fragrant. Add ② and chicken; cover and bring to boil. Reduce heat to medium and cook 15 minutes. Add ③ and continue to cook 5 minutes. Add evaporated milk then thicken with mixed ④ . May be served with rice or noodles.

五味鷄腿
Fried Flavored Chicken Legs

鷄腿 2 隻 ……… 1 斤（600 公克）
或鷄腿肉 2 隻 8 兩（300 公克）

① 鹽 ……………………… ¾ 小匙
胡椒 ……………………… 少許
蛋黃 …… 1 個或全蛋 …… ½ 個

太白粉 ………………… 5 大匙
炸油 …………………… 適量
沾汁 …………………… 適量

2 chicken legs, 1⅓ lbs.
(600g) or 2 boneless
chicken legs, ⅔ lb. (300g)

① ¾ t. salt
dash of pepper
1 egg yolk or ½ egg

5 T. cornstarch
oil for deep-frying
DIPPING SAUCE

1

2

1 若用帶骨鷄腿，可在中間直劃一刀，鷄肉攤開，較易炸熟。調上①料拌勻略醃，沾裹太白粉。

2 炸油燒熱，用中火將鷄腿炸至表面呈金黃色，皮脆肉熟（約 10 分鐘）。若用去骨鷄腿肉則炸約 8 分鐘，與沾汁配食。

沾汁（任選一）：

Ａ 芝麻醬或花生醬 2 大匙，徐徐拌入醬油 3 大匙，醋 2 大匙，再加糖 1 大匙，蔥、薑、蒜末各 1 小匙，辣油 ½ 大匙或辣椒醬 1 小匙拌勻。

Ｂ 醬油 2 大匙，檸檬汁 2 大匙，醋 1 大匙拌勻。亦可酌加蔥、薑、辣椒末、麻油及糖。

Ｃ 椒鹽（見 4 頁）1 小匙（圖 1）。　　**Ｄ** 辣醬油 1 大匙。

Ｅ 番茄醬 2 大匙或加芥末醬 1 小匙（圖 2）。

1 If chicken legs with bones are used, make vertical cuts to reveal bones then spread meat so it cooks easily and fast. Marinate chicken in ① . Coat chicken with cornstarch before deep-frying.

2 Heat oil to medium then deep-fry chicken 10 minutes or until golden brown, crispy and cooked. If boneless chicken legs are used, deep-fry 8 minutes. Remove and serve with dipping sauce.

DIPPING SAUCES (choose one of the following):

Ａ Gradually add 3 T. soy sauce and 2 T. vinegar to 2 T. sesame paste or peanut butter; stir to mix. Stir in 1 T. sugar; 1 t. each of minced green onions, ginger root, and garlic; ½ T. chili oil (or 1 t. hot pepper paste) and mix well.

Ｂ Mix 2 T. soy sauce, 2 T. lemon juice and 1 T. vinegar well. Chili pepper slices, sesame oil, sugar, minced green onions and ginger root may be added as desired.

Ｃ 1 t. Szechuan peppercorn salt (see p. 4) (Fig. 1).

Ｄ 1 T. hot soy sauce.

Ｅ 2 T. ketchup (1 t. mustard sauce may be added as desired) (Fig. 2).

芝麻鷄塊
Sesame Chicken

鷄肉…………8 兩（300 公克）

① { 酒、黑或白芝麻……各 1 大匙
　　鹽………………………½ 小匙

② { 蒜末、胡椒…………各少許
　　蛋……½ 個、太白粉……3 大匙

炸油……適量、檸檬……半個

沾汁（見左頁）…………適量

²⁄₃ lb. (300g) boneless
　　chicken

① { 1 T. each: wine, black or
　　　white sesame seeds
　　½ t. salt

② { 1 t. minced garlic
　　dash of pepper
　　½ egg, 3 T. cornstarch

oil for deep-frying, ½ lemon
DIPPING SAUCE (see p. 26)

1 鷄肉切約 12 大塊，拌入①、②料略醃。

2 炸油燒熱，將鷄肉用中火炸 3 分鐘，再改大火炸 3 分鐘至表面呈金黃色撈出。灑上檸檬汁，沾「沾汁」可與生菜沙拉（見 92 頁）共食。

1 Cut chicken into 12 pieces. Mix in ① and ② ; marinate.

2 Heat oil to medium then deep-fry chicken 4 minutes. Turn heat to high and continue to deep-fry 3 minutes or until golden brown; remove. Sprinkle with lemon juice then serve with dipping sauce. May also be served with "Mixed Lettuce Salad" (see p. 92).

炸大塊鷄
Fried Chicken

帶骨鷄胸或鷄腿（切大塊）1 斤
　　　　　　　　　（600 公克）

① { 酒…………………………1 大匙
　　鹽………………………¾ 小匙

② 料同上，炸油……………適量

沾汁（見左頁）…………適量

1⅓ lbs. (600g) chicken
　　breast or legs, cut into
　　pieces

① { 1 T. wine
　　¾ t. salt

② see ② in above recipe
oil for deep-frying
DIPPING SAUCE (see p. 26)

1 鷄塊拌入①、②料略醃。

2 炸油燒熱，將鷄塊用中火炸 6 分鐘，再改大火炸 4 分鐘，至表面呈金黃色撈出。沾「沾汁」可與「鮮菇奶果沙拉」（見 93 頁）共食。

1 Marinate chicken in ① , ② .

2 Heat oil to medium then deep-fry chicken 6 minutes. Turn heat high and continue to deep-fry 4 minutes or until golden brown; remove and serve with dipping sauce. May also be served with "Mushroom & Avocado Salad" (see p. 93).

紅燒鷄腿
Chicken Legs in Soy Sauce

鷄腿 2 隻 ……… 1 斤（600 公克）

香菇（泡軟切片）………… 4 朶

① { 紅蘿蔔 ………………………… ½ 杯
白蘿蔔或筍 ……………………… 1 杯

② { 酒 …… 3 大匙、醬油 …… ½ 杯
糖 ……………………………… ½ 大匙
胡椒或五香粉 ……………… ⅛ 小匙
（或花椒粒 ¼ 小匙或八角 ½ 朶）

③ { 太白粉 ………………………… 1 大匙
水 ………………………… 1½ 大匙

2　chicken legs, 1⅓ lbs. (600g)

4　chinese black mushrooms,
　　softened in water, sliced

① { ½ c. carrot
1　c. white radish or
　　bamboo shoots

② { 3　T. wine, ½ c. soy sauce
½ T. sugar
⅛ t. pepper or five-spice
　　powder (or ¼ t.
　　Szechuan peppercorns or
　　½ star anise)

③ { 1　T. cornstarch
1½ T. water

1　紅、白蘿蔔切塊（圖 1），用沸水煮熟約 5 分鐘。

2　鷄腿每隻約切 5 大塊（圖 2），加入②料，蓋鍋大火燒開後，改小火煮
　　15 分鐘；再加入香菇及①料煮 3 分鐘，煮時須翻拌，用③料勾成濃稠狀
　　即成。若火力太強，湯汁不夠時可酌量加水。

1　Cut carrot and white radish into pieces (Fig. 1) then cook in boiling
　　water 5 minutes.

2　Cut each chicken leg into 5 pieces (Fig. 2). Put chicken and ② in a
　　pot ; cover and bring to boil over high heat. Reduce heat to low;
　　cook 15 minutes. Add mushrooms and ① , cook 3 minutes; stir
　　during cooking. Mix ③ then add to thicken; remove and serve. Add
　　water if more liquid is needed.

椒鹽雞腿
Boiled Chicken Legs

雞腿 2 隻 ···· 1 斤（600 公克）
① { 酒 ······ 3 大匙、鹽 ····· 1½ 大匙
     花椒粒 ······················ ½ 大匙
沾汁：
{ 嫩薑絲 ·························· 1 大匙
  香菜、醬油 ··········· 各 2 大匙

2 chicken legs, 1⅓ lbs. (600g)
① { 3 T. wine, 1½ T. salt
     ½ T. Szechuan peppercorns
DIPPING SAUCE:
{ 1 T. shredded baby ginger
     root
  2 T. each: fresh coriander,
     soy sauce

1 雞腿用①料抹勻，醃 1 小時以上。煮時沖淨。

2 雞腿放入開水內（淹滿雞），大火煮開，再改用中火，蓋鍋煮約 30 分鐘至熟撈出。冰涼後切塊，沾「沾汁」。可與「炒青紅椒洋蔥」（見 91 頁）共食。

1 Marinate chicken in ① at least one hour; rinse before cooking.

2 Put chicken in boiling water (water should cover chicken); bring to boil. Reduce heat to medium; cover and cook 30 minutes. Remove chicken and let cool; refrigerate. Cut into pieces and serve with dipping sauce. May also be served with "Stir-fried Green, Red Peppers & Onion" (see p. 91), if desired.

醉雞腿
Chicken Legs in Wine

雞腿 2 隻 ···· 1 斤（600 公克）
① { 酒 ····························· ½ 杯
     鹽 ······· 1 小匙、胡椒 ······ 少許
沾汁：
{ 嫩薑絲、香菜 ········· 各 1 大匙
  醬油 ···· 2 大匙、麻油 ···· 1 小匙

2 chicken legs, 1⅓ lbs. (600g)
① { ½ c. wine, 1 t. salt
     dash of pepper
DIPPING SAUCE:
{ 1 T. each: fresh coriander,
     shredded baby ginger root
  2 T. soy sauce, 1 t. sesame oil

■ 參照上面做法 **2** 將雞煮熟後，整隻或切塊浸入拌勻的①料內（中途翻面）冰涼後，沾「沾汁」，可與「炒青梗菜」（見 91 頁）共食。

□ 煮雞汁留做「高湯」使用，雞腿可用蒸的需 30 分鐘，用微波爐需 8-10 分鐘。

■ Follow step **2** in above recipe to cook chicken legs. Marinate whole or cut chicken legs in ① , turn over during marinating. Serve with dipping sauce after refrigerating. May also be served with "Stir-fried Bok Choy" (see p. 91), if desired.

□ Reserve liquid from cooking for future use. Chicken legs may be steamed for 30 minutes or cooked in a microwave at high 8-10 minutes.

黑椒雞脯
Chicken Breast & Pepper

雞胸或雞腿肉 2 片 ……… 12 兩
（450 公克）
① { 黑胡椒 ………………… $\frac{1}{4}$ 小匙
  鹽 …………………… $\frac{1}{3}$ 小匙
蒜末 ……………………… 1 大匙
沙拉油或奶油 ………… 1 大匙

2 slices of boneless chicken
　breast or leg, 1 lb. (450g)
① { 1/4 t. black pepper
  1/3 t. salt
1 T. minced garlic
1 T. oil or butter

1 雞片用刀背略搥鬆，兩面撒上①料。

2 鍋燒熱加油 1 大匙，隨入雞片大火兩面各煎 2 分鐘，再改中火各煎約 2
分鐘呈金黃色，肉熟取出。餘油炒香蒜末，淋在雞脯上。可與蔬菜（見
88～95 頁）共食。

□ 可用烤箱 450°F ～500°F 烤 18 分鐘，撒上蒜末再烤 5 分鐘即可。

□ 豌豆莢選新鮮、豆粒小、顏色翠綠較佳(圖 1)。摘除老筋即可使用(圖 2)。

1 Use back of cleaver to tenderize chicken. Sprinkle ① on both sides of
chicken.

2 Heat pan, add 1 T. oil; fry each side of chicken slices over high heat for
2 minutes. Reduce heat to medium; fry each side 2 minutes until
golden brown and cooked. Remove chicken. Use remaining oil to stir-
fry garlic until fragrant then drizzle it over chicken. Serve with "vegetables (see pp. 88-95)" if desired.

□ If oven is used, bake chicken at 450°F-500°F 18 minutes. Sprinkle with
minced garlic and continue to roast 5 more minutes.

□ Fresh green Chinese pea pods with small peas (Fig. 1) should be used;
remove veins from both ends before using (Fig. 2).

番茄雞脯
Chicken Breast & Tomato

雞胸肉 2 片 12 兩（450 公克）
洋葱、番茄（切片）‥‥各 ½ 杯
① { 醬油、酒‥‥‥‥‥‥各 2 大匙
番茄醬‥‥3 大匙、糖‥‥2 小匙
水‥‥‥ ⅓ 杯、太白粉‥‥½ 小匙
洋菇、西芹（切片）‥‥各 ½ 杯

2　slices chicken breast,
　　1 lb. (450g)
½ c. each (sliced):
　　onion, tomato
① { 2　T. each: soy sauce, wine
3　T. ketchup, 2 t. sugar
⅓ c. water, ½ t. cornstarch
6　mushrooms, sliced
½ c. sliced celery

1 參照左頁做法 **1**、**2**，鹽減少爲 ¼ 小匙，將雞脯煎好切塊置盤。

2 鍋內餘油炒香洋葱，隨入番茄及①料，蓋鍋煮 2 分鐘，再加入洋菇及西芹蓋鍋煮 2 分鐘後，淋在雞脯上即成。

1 Follow steps **1** and **2** on p. 30, reducing salt to ¼ t., fry chicken until cooked. Cut into pieces.

2 Mix ① . Stir-fry onion in remaining oil until fragrant. Add tomato and ①; cover and cook 2 minutes. Add mushrooms and celery; cover and continue to cook 2 minutes. Pour mixture over chicken and serve.

乾椒雞脯
Spicy Chicken Breast

雞胸肉 2 片 ‥ 12 兩（450 公克）
① { 乾辣椒（切 1 公分長去籽） 1 支
蒜末‥‥1 小匙、麻油‥‥½ 大匙
② { 醬油、水‥‥‥‥‥各 2½ 大匙
糖、酒‥‥‥‥‥‥各 ½ 大匙
醋、太白粉‥‥‥‥‥各 1 小匙

2　slices of chicken breast,
　　1 lb. (450g)
① { 1　dried hot pepper, cut
　　to ½-inch long, remove
　　seeds
1　t. garlic, ½ T. sesame oil
② { 2½ T. each: soy sauce, water
½ T. each: sugar, wine
1　t. each: vinegar,
　　cornstarch

1 參照左頁做法 **1**、**2**，鹽減少爲 ¼ 小匙，將雞脯煎好。

2 鍋內餘油炒香①料，隨入②料拌成濃稠狀，淋在雞脯上，與「炒青花莢義大利瓜」（見 90 頁）共食。

☐ 若有現成的「宮保醬」3 大匙（見 6 頁）淋在煎好雞脯上即成。

1 Follow steps **1** and **2** on p. 30, reducing salt to ¼ t.; fry chicken until cooked.

2 Stir-fry ① in remaining oil until fragrant. Add ② and stir to thicken; pour sauce over chicken. Serve with "Stir-fried Broccoli & Zucchini" (see p. 90), if desired.

☐ 3 T. hot spicy sauce (see p. 6) may be substituted for sauce in step **2** to pour over chicken.

清炒雞丁
Stir-fried Shredded Chicken

① 雞肉丁（雞腿或雞胸）‥‥‥6 兩
（225 公克）
酒、醬油‥‥‥‥‥‥‥‥各 ½ 大匙
鹽‥‥‥‥‥‥‥‥‥‥‥‥ ¼ 小匙
胡椒‥‥‥‥‥‥‥‥‥‥‥‥ 少許
太白粉‥‥‥‥‥‥‥‥‥‥ ¾ 大匙
蔥（切 1 公分長）‥‥‥‥8 段

② 洋菇、蘆筍、紅蘿蔔切丁共1½ 杯

③ 酒‥‥‥‥‥‥‥‥‥‥‥‥ ½ 大匙
鹽、糖‥‥‥‥‥‥‥‥各 ⅓ 小匙
胡椒、麻油‥‥‥‥‥‥‥‥ 少許
太白粉‥‥‥‥‥‥‥‥‥‥ 1 小匙
水‥‥‥‥‥‥‥‥‥‥‥‥ 4 大匙

① ½ lb. (225g) boneless chicken leg or breast, shredded
½ T. each: wine, soy sauce
¼ t. salt
dash of pepper
¾ T. cornstarch
8 sections green onions, ½-inch long

② total of 1½ c. (diced): mushrooms, asparagus, carrot

③ ½ T. wine
⅓ t. each: salt, sugar
dash of pepper
sesame oil as desired
1 t. cornstarch
4 T. water

1 ①料拌勻，炒前拌入油 1 大匙，則炒時肉易分開。

2 油 1½ 大匙燒熱，放入雞丁炒至七分熟，鏟於一邊。餘油炒香蔥段，隨入②料略炒；再倒入③料，蓋鍋見有水蒸氣冒出拌炒均勻即成。

□ 雞去骨取肉、醃、炒法要領見 10～11 頁圖解。②料蔬菜可任選。

1 Mix ①. Add 1 T. oil before stir-frying so chicken shreds will separate easily during frying.

2 Heat 1½ T. oil; stir-fry ① until medium well then move to side of pan; stir-fry green onions in remaining oil. Add ② and stir briefly. Mix and add ③; cover and cook until steamy, then stir-fry to mix well.

□ To remove bones, marinate, and stir-fry the chicken, see pp. 10, 11. Other vegetables may be used to substitute for ingredients ②.

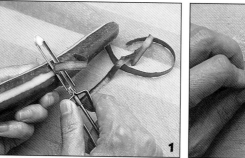
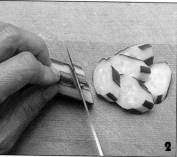

醬汁雞丁
Chicken & Soy Sauce

① 料同左

② { 葱（切1公分長）………10 段
蒜末、麻油…………各 ½ 大匙

③ 黃瓜、荸薺、紅椒丁··共 1 ½ 杯

④ { 醬油、水·………各 2 ½ 大匙
酒、糖、醋…………各 ½ 大匙
胡椒····少許、太白粉 …1 小匙

① see ① on p. 32

② { 10 sections green onions,
½-inch long
½ T. each: minced garlic,
sesame oil

③ { total of 1½ c. (diced):
cucumber, water
chestnuts, red pepper

④ { 2½ T. each: soy sauce, water
½ T. each: sugar, vinegar,
wine
dash of pepper
1 t. cornstarch

■ 參照左頁做法 **1**、**2**，將雞肉炒七分熟，鏟於一邊，餘油炒香②料，隨入③料略炒；再倒入④料，蓋鍋見有水蒸氣冒出拌炒均勻即成。

□ 小黃瓜亦可修條紋（圖 1），再切片（圖 2）較美觀。

■ Follow steps **1** and **2** on p. 32 to "... move to side of pan." Use remaining oil to stir-fry ② until fragrant. Add ③ and stir briefly. Mix and add ④ ; cover and cook until steamy, then stir to mix well.

□ To add beauty, cut thin strips on skin of cucumber (Fig. 1) then diagonally slice the cucumber (Fig. 2).

辣醬雞丁
Chicken & Hot Bean Paste

① 料同左

② { 辣豆瓣醬或辣椒醬………½ 大匙
葱、薑、蒜末、麻油 各 ½ 大匙

③ 豌豆莢、筍塊………共 1 ½ 杯

④ { 醬油、水·…………各 2 ½ 大匙
糖、酒…………………各 ½ 大匙
醋、太白粉…………各 1 小匙
胡椒………………………少許

① see ① on p. 32

② { ½ T. hot bean paste or hot
chili paste
½ T. each: sesame oil,
minced green onions,
ginger root, garlic

③ { total of 1½ c.: Chinese pea
pods, bamboo shoots

④ { 2½ T. each: soy sauce, water
½ T. each: sugar, wine
1 t. each: vinegar, cornstarch
dash of pepper

■ 參照左頁做法 **1**、**2**，將雞肉炒至七分熟，鏟於一邊。餘油炒香②料，隨入③料略炒；再倒入④料，蓋鍋見有水蒸氣冒出拌炒均勻即成。

□ 如有現成「魚香醬」（見 6 頁）6 大匙可取代②、④料較簡便。

■ Follow steps **1** and **2** on p. 32 to "... move to side of pan." Use remaining oil to stir-fry ② until fragrant. Add ③ and stir briefly. Mix and add ④ ; cover and cook until steamy, then stir to mix well.

□ 6 T. spicy Hunan sauce (see p. 6) may be substituted for ingredients ② and ④ .

宮保雞丁
Spicy Shredded Chicken

① 雞肉丁（雞腿或雞胸）……6 兩
　　　　　　　　　（225 公克）
　 酒、醬油……………… 各 ½ 大匙
　 鹽………………………… ¼ 小匙
　 胡椒……………………… 少許
　 太白粉……………………… ¾ 大匙

② 乾辣椒(切段去籽，圖 1)…1 支
　 蒜末、麻油………… 各 1 小匙

③ 絲瓜或義大利瓜丁
　 熟花生　　　　　　 共 1½ 杯

④ 醬油、水………… 各 2½ 大匙
　 糖、酒…………… 各 ½ 大匙
　 醋、太白粉………… 各 1 小匙

① ½ lb. (225g) boneless chicken
　　legs or breast, shredded
　½ T. each: wine, soy sauce
　¼ t. salt
　dash of pepper
　¾ T. cornstarch

② 1 dried hot pepper, cut into
　　½-inch long, remove
　　seeds (Fig. 1)
　1 t. minced garlic
　1 t. sesame oil

③ total of 1½ c. (diced): sponge-
　　gourd or squash, peanuts

④ 2½ T. each: soy sauce, water
　½ T. each: sugar, wine
　1 t. each: vinegar, cornstarch

1 ①料拌勻，炒前拌入油 1 大匙，則炒時肉易分開。

2 油 3 大匙燒熱，放入雞丁炒至七分熟，鏟於一邊。餘油炒香②料，隨入③料略炒；再倒入④料，蓋鍋見有水蒸氣冒出拌炒均勻即成。

☐ 如有現成「宮保醬」（見 6 頁）6 大匙可取代②、④料較簡便。

1 Mix ①. Add 1 T. oil before stir-frying so chicken shreds separate easily during frying.

2 Heat 3 T. oil; stir-fry ① until medium well then move to side of pan. Use remaining oil to stir-fry ② until fragrant. Add and stir ③ briefly. Mix and add ④ ; cover and cook until steamy, then stir to mix well.

☐ 6 T. hot spicy sauce (see p. 6) may be substituted for ingredients ② and ④.

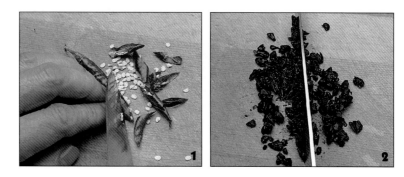

豉汁雞丁
Chicken &
Black Beans

① 料見左頁

②{ 蒜、豆豉（圖 2）剁碎‥1 大匙
　　葱、薑末各1小匙、麻油½大匙

③ 青紅椒、洋葱切丁……共 1½ 杯

④{ 醬油……1 大匙、鹽……⅙小匙
　　糖……½小匙、胡椒……少許
　　酒、太白粉…………各½大匙
　　水……………………⅓杯

① see ① on p. 34

②{ 1 T. each (minced): garlic,
　　fermented black beans
　　(Fig. 2)
　　1 t. each (minced):green
　　onions, ginger root
　　½ T. sesame oil

③{ total of 1½ c. (diced): green
　　& red peppers, onion

④{ 1 T. soy sauce, ⅙ t. salt
　　½ t. sugar, dash of pepper
　　½ T. each: wine, cornstarch
　　⅓ c. water

■ 參照左頁做法 **1**、**2**，將雞肉炒至七分熟，鏟於一邊。餘油炒香②料，隨入③料略炒；再倒入④料，蓋鍋見有水蒸氣冒出拌炒均勻即成。

■ Follow steps **1** and **2** on p. 34 to ."... move to side of pan." Use remaining oil to stir-fry ② until fragrant. Add and stir ③ briefly. Mix and add ④ ; cover and cook until steamy, then stir to mix well.

茄汁雞丁
Chicken &
Ketchup Sauce

① 料見左頁
　　葱末……2 大匙、蒜末……½大匙

②{ 西芹、洋葱
　　紅蘿蔔　}……切丁共1½杯

③{ 番茄醬……2 大匙、胡椒……少許
　　醬油、糖各½大匙、水 4 大匙
　　鹽…⅓小匙、太白粉…½大匙

① see ① on p. 34

　　2 T. minced green onions
　　½ T. minced garlic

②{ total of 1½ c. (diced):
　　celery, onion, carrot

③{ 2 T. ketchup, ⅓ t. salt
　　½ T. each: soy sauce, sugar
　　dash of pepper
　　½ T. cornstarch, 4 T. water

■ 參照左頁做法 **1**、**2**，將雞肉炒至七分熟，鏟於一邊。餘油炒香葱、蒜末，隨入②料略炒；再倒入③料，蓋鍋見有水蒸氣冒出拌炒均勻即成。

■ Follow steps **1** and **2** of "Stir-fried Chicken" (see p. 34) to "... move to side of pan." Use remaining oil to stir-fry green onions and garlic until fragrant. Add ② and stir briefly. Mix and add ③ ; cover and cook until steamy, then stir to mix well.

黑椒煎牛排
Steaks & Black Pepper

牛排 2 片 ………… 12 兩(450 公克)
或帶骨牛排 2 片…1 斤(600 公克)
鹽、黑胡椒……………… 各 $\frac{1}{3}$ 小匙
奶油…………………………1 大匙

2 boneless steaks, 1 lb.
(450g) or 2 steaks with
bone, 1¹/₃ lbs. (600g)
¹/₃ t. salt
¹/₃ t. black pepper
1 T. butter

1 牛排兩面撒上鹽、胡椒。

2 鍋燒熱,加沙拉油 1 大匙或使用牛排邊上的肥肉爆油使用(圖 1),牛排下鍋大火兩面各煎 1 分鐘呈金黃色(圖 2),再改用中火兩面各煎 2-3 分鐘(依需要的熟度調整煎牛排的時間),隨入奶油待溶化拌勻即可盛入盤內與「炒洋菇豌豆莢」(見 90 頁)共食。

☐ 如用烤箱以 500℉ 兩面各烤約 5-8 分鐘即可。

1 Sprinkle salt and pepper on both sides of steaks.

2 Heat 1 T. oil or steak fat (Fig. 1) then fry each side of steaks 1 minute or until golden brown (Fig. 2). Reduce heat to medium, fry each side of steaks 2-3 minutes (adjust frying time as desired). Add butter and mix well. Serve with "Stir-fried mushrooms & Chinese Pea Pods" (see p. 90).

☐ If oven is used, roast at 500°F 5-8 minutes on each side.

香蒜牛排
Garlic Flavored Steaks

牛排 2 片 ····· 12 兩（450 公克）
① ⎰ 蒜末·····················1 大匙
　 ⎱ 香菜末···················2 大匙
　 ⎱ 奶油····················1½ 大匙

2　steaks, 1 lb. (450g)
① ⎰ 1　T. minced garlic
　 ⎱ 2　T. minced coriander
　 ⎱ 1½ T. butter

1 參照左頁做法 **1**、**2** 煎牛排。

2 ①料炒香，淋在煎好的牛排上與「燙熟蘆筍」（見 88 頁）共食。

1 Follow steps **1**,**2** on p. 36 to fry steaks.

2 Stir-fry ① until fragrant then drizzle over fried steaks. Serve with "Boiled Asparagus" (see p. 88).

醬汁牛排
Steaks & Soy Sauce

牛排 2 片 ····· 12 兩（450 公克）
① ⎰ 酒、糖···············各½ 大匙
　 ⎱ 醬油·················1 大匙

2　steaks, 1 lb. (450g)
① ⎰ ½ T. each: wine, sugar
　 ⎱ 1　T. soy sauce

■ 參照左頁做法 **1**、**2** 煎牛排，唯鹽減為 $\frac{1}{8}$ 小匙，牛排煎好後大火加入①料迅速翻面即起鍋，汁淋在白飯上，與「炒四季豆紅蘿蔔」（見 90 頁）共食。

□ 亦可加入青蔥爆香。

■ Follow steps **1**,**2** on p. 36 to fry steaks, reducing salt to ⅛ t..Turn heat to high then add ① ; turn steaks over and remove immediately. Drizzle liquid from frying steaks over rice. Serve steaks with rice and "Stir-fried String Beans & Carrot" (see p. 90).

□ Green onions may be added and stir-fried until fragrant.

鐵板牛排
Steaks in Iron Plate

牛排 2 片 ····· 12 兩（450 公克）
或帶骨牛排2片1斤（600公克）
洋葱（切絲）················1 個
醬油、酒···········各 2 大匙
番茄醬··············1½ 大匙
① 糖、黑醋············各 1 大匙
水·····················½ 杯
太白粉·················½ 大匙

2　steaks, 1 lb. (450g)
　　or 2 steaks with bone,
　　1¹/₃ lbs. (600g)
1　onion, shredded
　2　T. each: soy sauce, wine
　1¹/₂T. ketchup
①　1　T. each: sugar,
　　　Worcestershire sauce
　¹/₂ c. water
　¹/₂ T. cornstarch

1 牛排兩面撒上鹽、胡椒各¼小匙。

2 鍋燒熱，加油 1 大匙，或使用牛排邊上的肥肉爆油使用，牛排下鍋大火兩面各煎 1 分鐘呈金黃色，再改中火兩面各煎 2-3 分鐘（依需要的熟度調整煎牛排的時間）。

3 油 2 大匙炒香洋葱呈金黃色（約 2 分鐘），隨入①料煮開成淋汁待用。

4 鐵板燒熱，放在木板模上，上置煎好的牛排，再灑上淋汁。

☐ 淋汁後立即蓋上蓋子可免濺油。

1 Sprinkle ¹/₄ t. each of salt and pepper on both sides of steaks.

2 Heat 1 T. oil or steak fat then fry each side of steak 1 minute or until golden brown. Reduce heat to medium, fry each side of steak 2-3 minutes (adjust frying time as desired).

3 Heat 2 T. oil then stir-fry onion until golden brown (about 2 minutes). Mix and add ① ; bring to boil to make sauce; remove.

4 Heat an iron plate, place on a wooden mold. Put steaks on iron plate then pour sauce over them.

☐ To avoid splashing when pouring sauce, cover plate and pour carefully.

薑檸汁牛排
Steaks in Juice

牛排 2 片 ‥ 12 兩（ 450 公克 ）
青葱花⋯⋯⋯⋯⋯⋯⋯⋯2 大匙
① ⎰ 薑末⋯⋯⋯⋯⋯⋯⋯⋯⋯1 大匙
　⎱ 檸檬汁、醬油⋯⋯⋯ 各 2 大匙
　⎱ 醋⋯⋯⋯⋯⋯⋯⋯⋯⋯½ 大匙

2　boneless steaks,
　　1 lb.(450g)
2　T. chopped green onions
1　T. minced ginger root
① ⎰ 2　T. each: lemon juice,
　　　　soy sauce
　⎱ ½ T. vinegar

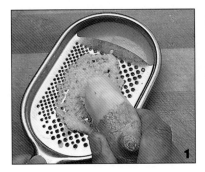

■　參照左頁做法 **1**、**2** 煎牛排，煎至半熟較嫩，切薄片置於盤內，撒上葱花，再淋上或沾①料即成。可與「炒青梗荣」（見 91 頁）共食。

□　薑最好用研磨器磨成泥狀（圖 1 ），若無剁碎亦可。

■　Follow steps **1**, **2** on p. 38 to fry steaks to medium rare. Slice steaks then place on a plate. Sprinkle with green onions and serve with dipping sauce. May also be served with "Stir-fried Bok Choy" (see p. 91).

□　It is preferable to use a grinder to grind ginger root (Fig. 1). If none is available, chop or mince ginger root.

煎牛排骨片
Fried Beef Ribs

牛排骨片 4 片 12 兩(450 公克)
① ⎰ 醬油⋯⋯⋯⋯⋯⋯⋯⋯3 大匙
　⎱ 糖、酒⋯⋯⋯⋯⋯⋯ 各 1 大匙

4　beef ribs, 1 lb. (450g)
① ⎰ 3　T. soy sauce
　⎱ 1　T. each: sugar, wine

1　牛排骨片切半成 8 片，調入①料醃半小時以上或隔夜。

2　油 2 大匙燒熱，放入牛排骨，中火兩面各煎約 2 分鐘呈金黃色肉熟，取出置盤與「炒菠荣」（見 90 頁）配食。

□　①料內可隨喜好加入蒜末或辣椒。

1　Cut ribs in half, making 8 ribs; marinate in ① at least 30 minutes or over night.

2　Heat 2 T. oil; fry ribs over medium heat until both sides are golden brown and cooked (about 2 minutes for each side). Remove and serve with "Stir-fried Spinach" (see p. 90).

□　Minced garlic or hot pepper may be added to ingredients ① if desired.

烤整塊牛排
Roast Beef Steak

菱眼或菲力牛排⋯⋯⋯⋯⋯ 1塊
　1斤半～2斤（900～1350公克）
酒⋯⋯⋯⋯⋯⋯⋯⋯⋯⋯ 2 大匙
鹽、黑胡椒⋯⋯⋯⋯⋯ 各¾ 小匙
棉線⋯⋯⋯⋯⋯⋯⋯⋯⋯⋯ 適量
① ⎰ 洋蔥（切片）⋯⋯⋯⋯⋯1個
　 ⎱ 西芹（切片）連葉⋯⋯⋯2 支
　⎧ 蠔油⋯⋯⋯⋯⋯⋯⋯⋯ 2 大匙
　⎪ 醬油⋯⋯⋯⋯⋯⋯⋯⋯ 1 大匙
② ⎨ 糖⋯⋯⋯⋯⋯⋯⋯⋯⋯ 1 小匙
　⎪ 胡椒⋯⋯⋯⋯⋯⋯⋯⋯ 少許
　⎩ 太白粉⋯⋯⋯⋯⋯⋯⋯ ¾ 大匙

1　rib eye or filet mignon
　　steak, 2-3 lbs. (900-1350g)
2　T. wine
³/₄ t. each: salt, pepper
cotton thread
① ⎰ 1 onion, sliced
　 ⎱ 2 celery stalks, sliced
　⎧ 2　T. oyster sauce
　⎪ 1　T. soy sauce
② ⎨ 1　t. sugar
　⎪ dash of pepper
　⎩ ³/₄ T. cornstarch

1 牛排表面先淋上酒，再撒上鹽、胡椒，用棉線捆緊，烤出的形狀較好。

2 備烤盤，上擺①料及牛排，淋油 2 大匙，用 350℉ 烤約 60-80 分鐘，烤時須翻面並淋水在肉上（水½杯分三次），依所需熟度調整烤的時間。

3 烤好的牛排稍待片刻後切片，分盛盤內，流出的肉汁與烤盤內餘汁加水成 1¼杯，調入②料，煮開成濃稠狀，淋在牛排上，與蔬菜（見 88-95 頁）配食。

1 Sprinkle wine, salt then pepper over steak. Wind thread around steak to secure.

2 Put ① and beef in a roasting pan; sprinkle with 2 T. oil. Roast at 350°F about 60-80 minutes; turn over several times during cooking; sprinkle with water (¹/₂ cup water can be used 3 times). Adjust roasting time according to tenderness desired.

3 Slice beef when slightly cool and place on a plate. Mix together juices extracted from slicing meat and from roasting pan; add water to make 1¹/₄ cups sauce. Mix and add in ② ; bring to boil and continue to cook until thick. Pour sauce over meat slices and serve with vegetable (see pp. 88-95).

椒麻牛排
Steak & Peppercorn

烤好的大牛排····約12 兩～1 斤
（見左頁）　（450～675 公克）
①
花椒粒（泡軟切碎）···· ½ 大匙
（或花椒粉············1 小匙）
葱末、醬油··········各 3 大匙
薑末···············1 大匙
糖、醋、麻油········各½ 大匙

roast steak for two (see p. 40),
1-1½ lbs. (450-675g)

①
½ T. Szechuan peppercorn,
soak to soften then chop
(or 1 t. Szechuan pepper-
corn powder)
3 T. minced green onions
1 T. minced ginger root
3 T. soy sauce
½ T. each: sugar, vinegar,
sesame oil

■ 烤好的整塊牛排切片置盤，上淋拌好的①料（圖 1 ），與「火腿粉絲沙拉」（見 94 頁）配食。

■ Slice the roast steak then place on plate. Mix and pour ① (Fig. 1) over steak and serve with "Ham & Bean Threads Salad" (p. 94).

1

烤牛大排骨
Roast Beef Ribs

牛大排骨 1 片····約 2 斤～3 斤
（1350～2250 公克）
①
海鮮醬或甜麵醬··········6 大匙
酒、醬油、糖··········各 4 大匙
蒜末·················1 大匙

1 slab of beef ribs, 3-5 lbs.
(1350-2250g)

①
6 T. Hoisin sauce or sweet
bean paste
4 T. each: wine, soy sauce
4 T. sugar
1 T. minced garlic

1 用刀劃開牛肋骨表層薄筋（食用時容易取肉），調入①料略醃（亦可加白芝麻 1 大匙）。

2 牛排骨置烤盤用 450°F 烤約 35-40 分鐘，至表面呈金黃色肉熟（中途翻面，並塗醃汁），在牛骨間隔處切開分食。

烤豬排骨　豬排骨 1 片（約 1 斤半～2 斤／900～1350 公克），½ 的①料，做法參照上面，烤約 30 分鐘。

1 Separate membrane of ribs with a knife; marinate in ① . 1 T. white sesame seeds may be added as desired.

2 Put ribs in a baking pan; reserve the marinade. Roast ribs at 450°F 35-40 minutes or until cooked and golden brown; turn ribs over and spread with marinade during roasting. Cut between bones and serve.

ROAST PORK RIBS　Use one slab of pork back ribs (2-3 lbs./900-1350g) and half portion of ingredients ① ; follow procedures in above recipe and roast 30 minutes.

番茄牛肉
Beef & Tomato in Soy Sauce

牛肉(切塊)1斤4兩(750公克)
(紅燒用腿肉、肋條、牛腩均可)

① { 洋葱、番茄各1個 | 紅蘿蔔………1條 } 切塊(圖1)

② { 酒、番茄醬…………各3大匙 | 醬油………………………4大匙 | 糖………………………2小匙 | 胡椒………………………少許 }

③ { 水………………………2大匙 | 太白粉…………………1⅓大匙 }

$1^2/_3$ lbs. (750g) beef, cut into pieces

① { 1 each (cut into pieces, Fig.1): onion, tomato, carrot }

② { 3 T. wine | 4 T. soy sauce | 3 T. ketchup | 2 t. sugar | dash of pepper }

③ { 2 T. water | $1^1/_3$ T. cornstarch }

1

■ 油2大匙燒熱，先將①料內洋葱炒香，再下番茄略炒；隨入牛肉、紅蘿蔔、②料及水1杯燒開後，改小火煮約1小時至肉軟，汁剩約⅔時，以③料勾芡即成。此道菜很適合與熟麵配食。

使用烤箱
■ 依照上法將牛肉等材料加水（水1杯改爲½杯）燒開，以③料勾芡，盛入烤盆加蓋用375°-400°F烤1小時。烤盆放在加水的烤盤中。

■ Heat 2 T. oil then stir-fry onion of ① until fragrant; add tomato and stir briefly. Add beef, carrot, ②, and 1 cup water; bring to boil. Reduce heat to low and cook 1 hour or until meat is tender and liquid reduced to $^2/_3$; thicken with mixed ③. This dish is suitable to serve with cooked noodles.

ROASTING IN AN OVEN:

1 Follow above procedure to cook beef, ①, ② with water (reduce water from 1 cup to $^1/_2$ cup); bring to boil then thicken with ③. Put mixture in a baking dish and cover.

2 Place the baking dish in a properly water-filled baking pan; roast at 375°F-400°F 1 hour.

番茄牛尾
Oxtails &
Tomato

牛尾（切大塊）⋯⋯⋯約 2 斤
　　　　（900～1350 公克）
①、②、③料同左
水⋯⋯⋯⋯⋯⋯⋯⋯⋯ 1½ 杯

2-3 lbs. (900-1350g) oxtails,
　cut into large pieces
①, ②, ③ see ①, ②, ③ on p. 42
1½ c. water

■ 做法參照左頁，唯煮的時間改爲 80 分鐘至牛尾熟爛。

■ Follow procedures on p. 42, but increase cooking time to 80 minutes.

番茄雞腿
Chicken Legs &
Tomato

雞腿（切大塊）約2斤（900公克）
①、②、③料同左
水（紅燒用）⋯⋯⋯⋯⋯1 杯

2 lbs. (900g) chicken legs,
　cut into large pieces
①, ②, ③ see ①, ②, ③ on p. 42
1 c. water

■ 做法參照左頁，唯煮的時間改爲 40 分鐘至雞肉熟。也可續加洋菇、西芹再煮 2 分鐘後勾芡。

■ Follow procedures on p. 42, except reduce cooking time to 40 minutes. Mushrooms and celery may be added; cook 2 more minutes then thicken with mixed cornstarch and water.

糖醋牛排骨
Sweet & Sour Beef Ribs

牛排骨片……9 兩（340 公克）

① 酒、醬油……………各 ¾ 大匙
蛋黃…… 1 個或蛋…… ½ 個

太白粉………………3 大匙

炸油…………………適量

葱、蒜末…………各 1 小匙

② 洋葱、西芹、紅椒 切塊共 1 杯

③ 醬油、糖、醋……各 2¾ 大匙
水………………………½ 杯
太白粉………………½ 大匙

³/₄ lb. (340g) beef ribs

① ³/₄ T. each: wine, soy sauce
1 egg yolk or ½ egg

3 T. cornstarch

oil for deep-frying

1 t. each: minced green
onions, garlic

② total of 1 c. (cut into pieces):
onion, celery, red pepper

③ 2 ³/₄ T. each: soy sauce,
sugar, vinegar
½ c. water
½ T. cornstarch

1️⃣ 牛排骨在骨與骨的間隔處切開成約 7 公分長方片（圖 1），調入①料，炸前再拌上太白粉。

2️⃣ 炸油燒熱，放入牛排骨大火炸熟約 4 分鐘撈出。

3️⃣ 油 2 大匙燒熱，炒香葱、蒜末，隨入②料略炒，再加③料煮沸後，續入炸過的牛排骨拌炒均勻。

☐ 若有現成的糖醋醬（四種口味見 7 頁）可隨嗜好任選 1 杯來取代③料。

☐ 任何蔬菜可選用來取代②料。

1️⃣ Cut ribs into 3-inch long pieces by cutting between each rib (Fig. 1); mix with ① . Coat each piece with cornstarch before deep-frying.

2️⃣ Heat oil then deep-fry ribs over high heat about 4 minutes; remove.

3️⃣ Heat 2 T. oil; stir-fry green onions and garlic. Add ② and stir briefly. Mix and add ③ ; bring to boil. Add ribs; stir-fry to mix well. Serve.

☐ A cup of any sweet & sour sauce on p. 7 may be substituted for ingredients ③ .

☐ Other vegetables may be substituted for ingredients ② .

1

糖醋排骨
Sweet & Sour Pork Ribs

豬小排骨（切小塊）⋯⋯⋯9 兩
　　　　　　　　（340 公克）

①、②料同左
　　太白粉⋯⋯3 大匙、炸油⋯適量
　　葱、蒜末⋯⋯⋯⋯⋯⋯各 1 小匙

③ ┤ 鳳梨(切小丁) $\frac{1}{2}$ 杯、鹽 $\frac{1}{2}$ 小匙
　　鳳梨汁、糖⋯⋯⋯⋯各 4 大匙
　　醋⋯3 大匙、太白粉⋯ $\frac{1}{2}$ 大匙

$^3/_4$ lb. (340g) pork back ribs

①, ② see ①, ② on p. 44

　　3 T. cornstarch
　　oil for deep-frying
　　1 t. each: minced green
　　　　onions, garlic

③ ┤ $\frac{1}{2}$ c. diced pineapple
　　$\frac{1}{2}$ t. salt
　　4 T. each: pineapple juice,
　　　　sugar
　　3 T. vinegar, $\frac{1}{2}$ T. cornstarch

■ 參照糖醋牛排骨做法，唯炸的時間加長為 6 分鐘。

☐ 若有現成的糖醋醬（見 7 頁）可隨嗜好任選 1 杯來取代③料。

☐ 紅蘿蔔及義大利瓜（或絲瓜）切塊或其他蔬菜可取代②料。鳳梨可用新鮮或罐頭。

■ Follow procedures on p. 44, but increase deep-frying time to 6 minutes.

☐ A cup of any sweet & sour sauce on p. 7 may be substituted for ingredients ③.

☐ Carrot and zucchini (or sponge-gourd), cut into pieces, or other vegetables may be substituted for ② . Fresh or canned pineapple may be used.

糖醋里肌
Sweet & Sour Tenderloin

豬或牛里肌肉(切片)⋯⋯⋯6 兩
　　　　　　　　（225 公克）

①、②料同左
　　太白粉⋯⋯2 大匙、炸油⋯適量
　　葱、蒜末⋯⋯⋯⋯⋯各 1 小匙

③ ┤ 番茄醬、醋⋯⋯⋯⋯各 $2\frac{1}{2}$ 大匙
　　糖、水⋯⋯⋯⋯⋯⋯各 3 大匙
　　鹽⋯ $\frac{2}{5}$ 小匙、太白粉⋯ $\frac{1}{2}$ 大匙

$\frac{1}{2}$ lb. (225g) pork or beef tenderloin, sliced

①, ② see ① , ② on p. 44

　　2 T. cornstarch
　　oil for deep-frying
　　1 t. each: minced green
　　　　onions, garlic

③ ┤ $2\frac{1}{2}$ T. each: ketchup, vinegar
　　3 T. each: sugar, water
　　$^2/_5$ t. salt, $\frac{1}{2}$ T. cornstarch

■ 參照糖醋牛排骨做法，唯炸的時間縮短為 3 分鐘。

☐ 若有現成的糖醋醬（見 7 頁）可任選 1 杯來取代③料。

☐ 番茄、小黃瓜及木耳切片或其他蔬菜可取代②料。

■ Follow procedures on p. 44, but reduce deep-frying time to 3 minutes.

☐ A cup of any sweet & sour sauce on p. 7 may be substituted for ingredients ③.

☐ Sliced tomato, cucumber, and wood ears (or other vegetables) may be substituted for ② .

糖醋丸子
Sweet & Sour Meat Balls

豬或牛絞肉　8 兩（300 公克）

① 酒、太白粉、麵粉‥‥各 1 大匙
蛋‥‥‥‥ $\frac{1}{2}$ 個或水‥‥‥‥2 大匙
鹽‥‥‥‥‥‥‥‥‥‥ $\frac{1}{3}$ 小匙
洋葱末‥‥‥‥‥‥‥‥‥3 大匙
炸油‥‥‥‥‥‥‥‥‥‥‥適量

② 小紅蘿蔔、洋菇、青花菜　切片‥1 杯

③ 醬油、糖、醋‥‥‥各 2 $\frac{3}{4}$ 大匙
水‥‥ $\frac{1}{2}$ 杯、太白粉‥‥ $\frac{1}{2}$ 大匙

$^2/_3$ lb. (300g) ground pork or beef

① 1 T. each: wine, cornstarch, flour
$^1/_2$ egg or 2 T. water
$^1/_3$ t. salt
3 T. minced onion
oil for deep-frying

② total of 1 c. (sliced):
small carrot, mushrooms, broccoli

③ 2$^3/_4$T. each: soy sauce, sugar, vinegar
$^1/_2$ c. water
$^1/_2$ T. cornstarch

1 絞肉調入①料，拌勻至有黏性（圖 1），擠成丸子（圖 2）放入燒熱炸油內炸熟（約 5 分鐘）。

2 油 2 大匙略炒②料，隨入③料，煮開後續入炸熟丸子拌勻即可。

☐ 糖醋醬（見 7 頁）可任選 1 杯來取代③料。

1 Mix ground pork with ① ; stir until sticky (Fig. 1). Manually form meat into meat balls (Fig.2). Heat oil then deep-fry meat balls until cooked (about 5 minutes).

2 Heat 2 T. oil; stir-fry ② until cooked. Mix and add ③ ; bring to boil. Add meat balls and mix well.

☐ A cup of any sweet & sour sauce on p. 7 may be substituted for ingredients ③ .

糖醋魚排
Sweet & Sour Fish Fillets

魚淨肉⋯⋯⋯ 8 兩（300 公克）

① { 酒⋯⋯ ½ 大匙、鹽⋯⋯ ⅓ 小匙
蛋黃⋯⋯⋯ 1 個或蛋⋯⋯ ½ 個

太白粉⋯ 3 大匙、炸油⋯ 適量

② { 洋葱、香菇
青、紅椒 } 切片⋯⋯⋯ 1½ 杯

③ { 番茄醬、醋⋯⋯⋯⋯ 各 2½ 大匙
糖、水⋯⋯⋯⋯⋯⋯ 各 3 大匙
鹽⋯ ⅖ 小匙、太白粉⋯ ½ 大匙

⅔ lb. (300g) fish meat

① { ½ T. wine, ⅓ t. salt
1 egg yolk or ½ egg

3 T. cornstarch
oil for deep-frying

② { total of 1½ c. (sliced):
onion, green & red peppers,
Chinese black mushrooms

③ { 2½ T. each: ketchup, vinegar
3 T. each: sugar, water
⅖ t. salt, ½ T. cornstarch

1 魚肉斜片成 6～8 片，調①料拌勻，炸前沾上太白粉，油燒熱，將魚片放入炸油內炸熟約 3 分鐘，呈金黃色肉熟撈出置盤。

2 油 2 大匙略炒②料隨入③料燒開，澆淋在炸好的魚片上。

☐ 糖醋醬（見 7 頁）可任選 1 杯取代③料。

1 Slant the knife to slice meat into 6-8 fillets then mix with ① ; coat with cornstarch before deep-frying. Heat oil then deep-fry fillets until cooked and golden brown (about 3 minutes); remove.

2 Heat 2 T. oil then stir-fry ② briefly. Mix and add ③ ; bring to boil. Pour sauce over fillets and serve.

☐ A cup of any sweet & sour sauce on p. 7 may be substituted for ingredients ③.

檸檬鷄片
Chicken Slices & Lemon

鷄胸肉⋯⋯⋯ 8 兩（300 公克）

① { 同上①料
太白粉⋯⋯⋯⋯⋯⋯ 1 大匙

炸油適量、②料同上

③ { 檸檬（切薄片）⋯⋯⋯⋯ 半個
檸檬汁、糖⋯⋯⋯⋯ 各 4 大匙
水⋯⋯⋯ ½ 杯、鹽⋯⋯ ½ 小匙
太白粉⋯⋯⋯⋯⋯⋯⋯ ½ 大匙

⅔ lb. (300g) chicken breast

① { see ① in above recipe
1 T. cornstarch

oil for deep-frying

② see ② in above recipe

③ { ½ lemon, sliced
4 T. each: lemon juice, sugar
½ c. water, ½ t. salt
½ T. cornstarch

1 鷄肉切薄片調①料拌勻，炸油燒熱用小火炸約 1½ 分鐘至剛熟即可撈出。

2 油 2 大匙略炒②料取出置盤。③料燒開，入炸熟鷄片拌勻置蔬菜上。

☐ 糖醋醬（見 7 頁）可任選 1 杯取代③料。

☐ 紅蘿蔔、洋菇及豌豆莢切片，或其他蔬菜可取代②料。

1 Cut chicken into thin slices then mix with ① . Heat oil then deep-fry chicken over low heat until cooked (about 1½ minutes); remove.

2 Heat 2 T. oil then stir-fry ② until cooked; remove. Mix ③ and bring to boil. Add chicken slices and mix; remove and put on vegetables.

☐ A cup of any sweet & sour sauce on p. 7 for ingredients ③ .

☐ Carrot, mushrooms, and Chinese pea pods may be substituted for ②.

蠔油牛肉
Beef & Oyster Sauce

牛肉（見 12 頁 **4**）………6 兩
　　　　（ 225 公克）
① { 醬油、酒……………各 1 大匙
　　太白粉、水…………各 1 大匙
葱、薑末………………½ 大匙
蘆筍……………………1½ 杯
② { 醬油、蠔油…………各 1 大匙
　　（或醬油…………2 大匙）
　　酒、糖、太白粉……各 ½ 大匙
　　胡椒、麻油……………少許
　　水……………………4 大匙
芝麻（無亦可）………½ 大匙

½ lb. (225g) beef flank
　(see p. 12, **4**)
① { 1 T. each: soy sauce, wine
　　1 T. each: cornstarch, water
½ T. minced green onions &
　ginger root
1½ c. asparagus
② { 1 T. each: soy sauce, oyster
　　　sauce (or 2 T. soy sauce)
　　½ T. each: wine, sugar,
　　　cornstarch
　　dash of pepper
　　4 T. water
　　sesame oil as desired
½ T. sesame seeds (optional)

1 牛肉順紋先切 5 公分寬長條（圖 1），再切薄片（圖 2），調①料，炒前拌入油 1 大匙，則炒時肉易分開。

2 油 1½ 大匙燒熱，放入牛肉炒至六分熟取出，餘油炒香葱、薑、蘆筍；再倒入②料及牛肉，蓋鍋見有水氣冒出拌炒均勻撒上芝麻。

□ 牛肉醃、炒要領見 10～11 頁圖解。

□ 任何蔬菜可選用來取代蘆筍。

1 Cut beef into 2-inch wide strips along grain (Fig. 1), then slice across the grain (Fig. 2); mix in ①. Mix 1 T. oil with beef before frying so beef will separate easily during frying.

2 Heat 1½ T. oil then stir-fry beef until medium well; remove. Use remaining oil to stir-fry green onions, ginger root, and asparagus until fragrant. Add mixed ② and beef. Cover and cook until steamy, then stir-fry to mix well. Remove, sprinkle with sesame seeds and serve.

□ Tips for marinating and frying are shown in figures on pp. 10-11.

□ Other vegetables may be substituted for asparagus.

西芹牛肉
Beef & Celery

牛肉………… 6 兩（ 225 公克 ）
① 料同左
② { 乾辣椒(切1公分長去籽) ½ 大匙
蒜末…… 1 小匙、麻油 … ½ 大匙
③ 西芹、洋菇…… 切片共約 1½ 杯
④ { 醬油、水………… 各 2½ 大匙
糖、酒………………… 各 ½ 大匙
醋、太白粉………… 各 1 小匙

½ lb. (225g) beef
① see ① on p. 48
② {
½ T. dried hot pepper, cut
　　into 2-inch long, remove
　　seeds
1　t. minced garlic
½ T. sesame oil
③ {
total of 1½ c. (sliced):
　　celery, mushrooms
④ {
2½ T. each: soy sauce, water
½ T. each: sugar, wine
1　t. each: vinegar, cornstarch

■ 參照左頁做法 **1**、**2**，將牛肉炒至六分熟取出。餘油炒香②料，隨入③料略炒；再倒入④料及牛肉，蓋鍋見有水氣冒出拌炒均勻。

□ 如有現成「宮保醬」（見 6 頁）6 大匙，可取代②、④料較簡便。

■ Follow steps **1** and **2** on p. 48 to stir-fry beef until medium well; remove. Stir-fry ② in remaining oil until fragrant. Add ③ and stir briefly. Add mixed ④ and beef. Cover and cook until steamy then stir-fry to mix well. Remove and serve.

□ 6 T. hot spicy sauce (see p. 6) may be substituted for ingredients ② and ④ .

豉椒牛肉
Beef &
Black Beans

牛肉………… 6 兩(225 公克)
① 料同左
② { 豆豉（ 剁碎 ）…………… 1 大匙
葱、薑、蒜末、麻油 各 ½ 大匙
③ 洋葱、青紅椒…… 切片共 1½ 杯
④ { 醬油…… 1 大匙、鹽…… ⅙ 小匙
糖… ½ 小匙、胡椒…… 少許
酒、太白粉各 1 小匙、水 5 大匙

½ lb. (225g) beef
① see ① on p. 48
② {
1　T. minced fermented
　　black beans
½ T. each: sesame oil,
　　minced garlic, green
　　onions, ginger root
③ {
total of 1½ c. (sliced): onion,
　　green & red peppers
④ {
1　T. soy sauce, ⅙ t. salt
½ t. sugar, 5 T. water
dash of pepper
1　t. each: wine, cornstarch

■ 參照左頁做法 **1**、**2**，將牛肉炒至六分熟取出。餘油炒香②料，隨入③料略炒；再入④料及牛肉，蓋鍋見有水蒸氣冒出拌炒均勻。

□ 如有現成「豉汁醬」（見 6 頁）6 大匙，可取代②、④料較簡便。

■ Follow steps **1** and **2** on p. 48 to stir-fry beef until medium well; remove. Use remaining oil to stir-fry ② until fragrant. Add ③ and stir briefly. Add mixed ④ and beef. Cover and cook until steamy, then stir to mix well. Remove and serve.

□ 6 T. black beans sauce (see p. 6) may be substituted for ingredients ② and ④ .

茄汁牛肉
Beef & Ketchup Sauce

牛肉⋯⋯⋯⋯6 兩（225 公克）

① { 醬油、酒⋯⋯⋯⋯⋯ 各 1 大匙
太白粉、水⋯⋯⋯⋯ 各 1 大匙

② 洋蔥、番茄、青椒切片 1½ 杯（圖 1）

③ { 番茄醬⋯⋯⋯⋯⋯⋯3 大匙
醬油、糖⋯⋯⋯⋯⋯ 各 ½ 大匙
鹽⋯⋯ ⅓ 小匙、水 ⋯ 4 大匙
太白粉⋯⋯⋯⋯⋯⋯1 小匙

½ lb. (225g) beef

① { 1 T. each: soy sauce, wine
1 T. each: cornstarch, water

② { total of 1½ c. (sliced):
onion, tomato, green
pepper (Fig. 1)

③ { 3 T. ketchup
½ T. each: soy sauce, sugar
⅓ t. salt, 4 T. water
1 t. cornstarch

1 牛肉順紋先切 5 公分長條，再切薄片，調①料，炒前拌入油 1 大匙，則炒時肉易分開。

2 油 1½ 大匙燒熱，放入牛肉炒至六分熟取出，餘油略炒②料，隨入③料及牛肉；蓋鍋見有水蒸氣冒出拌炒均勻。

1 Cut beef into 2-inch wide strips along grain, then slice across the grain; mix in ① . Mix 1 T. oil with beef before frying so beef will separate easily during frying.

2 Heat 1½ T. oil then stir-fry beef until medium well; remove. Use remaining oil to stir-fry ② . Add ③ and beef. Cover and cook until steamy; stir to mix well.

咖哩牛肉
Curry Beef

牛肉…………6 兩（225 公克）
①、②料見左頁
③ { 咖哩粉、酒…………各 1 大匙
鹽、糖………………各 $\frac{1}{2}$ 小匙
水…… 4 大匙、太白粉…… 1 小匙

$\frac{1}{2}$ lb (225g) beef
①, ② see ① , ② on p. 50
③ {
1 T. each: curry powder, wine
$\frac{1}{2}$ t. each: salt, sugar
4 T. water
1 t. cornstarch

■ 參照左頁做法 **1**、**2**，將牛肉炒至六分熟取出，餘油略炒②料；隨入③料
及牛肉，蓋鍋見有水蒸氣冒出拌炒均勻即可。

□ 青花菜、洋葱及洋菇切片共 1$\frac{1}{2}$ 杯或其他蔬菜可取代②料。

■ Follow steps **1** and **2** on p. 50 to stir-fry beef until medium well;
remove. Use remaining oil to stir-fry ② briefly. Add mixed ③ and beef.
Cover and cook until steamy; stir to mix well. Remove and serve.

□ Sliced broccoli, onion, and mushrooms (or other vegetables) may be
substituted for ② .

沙茶牛肉
Beef &
Barbecue Sauce

牛肉…………6 兩（225 公克）
① 料見左頁
② { 沙茶醬、醬油………各 1$\frac{1}{2}$ 大匙
酒、糖、太白粉……各 $\frac{1}{2}$ 大匙
水…………………… 4 大匙

$\frac{1}{2}$ lb. (225g) beef
① see ① on p. 50
② {
1$\frac{1}{2}$T. barbecue (Sa Tsa) sauce
1$\frac{1}{2}$T. soy sauce, 4 T. water
$\frac{1}{2}$ T. each: wine, sugar,
cornstarch

■ 參照左頁做法 **1**、**2**，將牛肉炒至六分熟，隨入②料炒勻，放在已炒好豌
豆莢上（見 90 頁）。

■ Follow steps **1** and **2** on p. 50 to stir-fry beef until medium well. Mix
then add ② ; stir-fry until cooked; put beef over fried pea pods (see
p. 90) and serve.

煎豬排
Fried Pork Chops

豬大排或豬里肌肉 2 片 ····8 兩
（300 公克）

鹽····················¼ 小匙

胡椒····················少許

① ┌ 洋葱（切絲）············1 個
　├ 蒜末····················1 大匙
　└ 洋菇（切片）············6 粒

② ┌ 酒····················2 大匙
　├ 醬油····················3 大匙
　└ 糖····················½ 大匙

2 pork chops or tenderloin,
  ²/₃ lb. (300g)

¼ t. salt

dash of pepper

① ┌ 1 onion, shredded
　├ 1 T. minced garlic
　└ 6 mushrooms, sliced

② ┌ 2 T. wine
　├ 3 T. soy sauce
　└ ½ T. sugar

1 豬排切斷邊緣筋部，用刀背拍鬆，兩面撒上鹽、胡椒。

2 鍋燒熱，油 1 大匙淋勻鍋面，隨入豬排，大火兩面各煎 1 分鐘使呈金黃色；改中火再各煎約 1½ 分鐘至肉熟取出。

3 油 1 大匙炒香①料，隨入②料煮開，澆在煎好的豬排上。可與「燙熟韭菜」（見 89 頁）共食。

□ 新鮮洋菇選色白、傘部沒打開者為佳（見圖 1、2）。

1 Cut the tendons on rim of pork. Tenderize pork with a meat mallet. Sprinkle salt and pepper on both sides.

2 Heat pan then add 1 T. oil. Fry pork over high heat, about 1 minute for each side, until golden brown. Reduce heat to medium and continue to fry, about 1½ minutes on each side, until cooked.

3 Heat 1 T. oil. Stir-fry ① until fragrant. Add ② and bring to boil then pour over pork. May be served with "boiled Chinese leeks" (see p. 89).

□ Fresh mushrooms with whiter color and not split around the stem (Figs. 1, 2) should be used.

茄汁豬排
Pork Chops
& Ketchup Sauce

豬大排或豬里肌肉⋯⋯⋯⋯8 兩
（300 公克）

鹽⋯⋯⋯ $\frac{1}{4}$ 小匙、胡椒⋯⋯少許

① 料同左頁

②
醬油、酒⋯⋯⋯⋯⋯⋯各 2 大匙
番茄醬⋯⋯⋯⋯⋯⋯⋯ 2 $\frac{1}{2}$ 大匙
糖⋯⋯⋯1 大匙、醋⋯⋯ $\frac{2}{3}$ 大匙
水⋯⋯ $\frac{1}{2}$ 杯、太白粉⋯⋯ $\frac{1}{2}$ 大匙

$\frac{2}{3}$ lb. (300g) pork chops or
tenderloin

$\frac{1}{4}$ t. salt, dash of pepper

① see ① on p. 52

②
2　T. each: soy sauce, wine
2$\frac{1}{2}$ T. ketchup
1　T. sugar, $\frac{1}{2}$ c. water
$\frac{2}{3}$ T. vinegar
$\frac{1}{2}$ T. cornstarch

■ 做法參照左頁 **1**、**2**、**3** 與「燙熟芥蘭菜」（見 88 頁）共食。

豉汁豬排　①料略炒，加入豉汁醬（見 6 頁）6 大匙拌炒，淋在煎好的豬
排上。

宮保豬排　①料略炒，加入宮保醬（見 6 頁）6 大匙拌炒，淋在煎好的豬
排上。

■ Follow steps **1** , **2** and **3** on p. 52 and serve with "boiled broccoli"
(see p. 88).

PORK CHOPS & BLACK BEAN SAUCE Heat 1 T. oil and stir-fry ① until
cooked. Add 6 T. black bean sauce (see p. 6) and stir-fry until mixed
well. Pour sauce over pork.

SPICY PORK CHOPS Heat 1 T. oil and stir-fry ① until cooked. Add 6 T. hot
spicy sauce (see p. 6) and stir-fry until mixed well. Pour sauce over
pork.

鳳梨豬排
Pork Chops &
Pineapple

豬大排 ⋯⋯⋯ 8 兩（300 公克）

鹽⋯⋯⋯ $\frac{1}{4}$ 小匙、胡椒⋯⋯少許

① 料同左頁

②
新鮮或罐裝鳳梨丁⋯⋯⋯⋯ $\frac{1}{2}$ 杯
鳳梨汁、糖⋯⋯⋯⋯⋯各 4 大匙
醋⋯⋯3 大匙、鹽⋯⋯⋯ $\frac{1}{3}$ 小匙
太白粉⋯⋯⋯⋯⋯⋯⋯⋯ $\frac{1}{2}$ 大匙

$\frac{2}{3}$ lb. (300g) pork chops

$\frac{1}{4}$ t. salt, dash of pepper

① see ① on p. 52

②
$\frac{1}{2}$ c. fresh or canned
pineapple, diced
4　T. each: pineapple juice,
sugar
3　T. vinegar, $\frac{1}{3}$ t. salt
$\frac{1}{2}$ T. cornstarch

■ 參照左頁做法 **1**、**2**、**3** 與燙熟「義大利瓜、蘆筍」（見 88 頁）共食。

■ Follow steps **1** , **2** and **3** on p. 52 and serve with boiled zucchini
and asparagus (see p. 88).

炸豬排
Deep-fried Pork Chops

豬大排或豬里肌肉 2 片 ⋯⋯8 兩
（300 公克）

① 醬油、酒⋯⋯⋯⋯⋯⋯ 各 $\frac{1}{2}$ 大匙
糖⋯⋯1 小匙、鹽⋯⋯ $\frac{1}{3}$ 小匙
胡椒或五香粉⋯⋯⋯⋯⋯⋯ 少許
蒜末⋯⋯⋯⋯⋯⋯⋯⋯ $\frac{1}{2}$ 大匙
蛋黃⋯⋯ 1 個或蛋⋯⋯ $\frac{1}{2}$ 個

太白粉⋯⋯⋯⋯⋯⋯⋯⋯ 3 大匙
炸油⋯⋯⋯⋯⋯⋯⋯⋯⋯ 適量
沾汁：椒鹽（見 4 頁）⋯1 小匙
或番茄醬 2 大匙、芥末醬 1
小匙拌勻

2 pork chops or tenderloin,
   $^{2}/_{3}$ lb. (300g)

① ½ T. each: soy sauce, wine
   1 t. sugar, $^{1}/_{3}$ t. salt
   dash of pepper or five-spice
      powder
   ½ T. minced garlic
   1 egg yolk or ½ egg

3 T. cornstarch
oil for deep-frying
DIPPING SAUCE:
1 t. Szechuan peppercorn
   salt (see p. 4) (or 2 T.
   ketchup and 1 t. mustard
   sauce mixed together)

1 豬排用刀背搥鬆，調入①料拌勻略醃，炸前拌入太白粉 3 大匙。

2 炸油燒熱，大火將豬排炸熟至金黃色（約 4 分鐘）撈起置盤，沾「沾汁」與「雞絲沙拉」（見 92 頁）共食。

五味汁豬排　醬油、蔥、水各 2 大匙，辣椒、蒜、薑末、糖、麻油各 1 小匙，醋 $\frac{1}{2}$ 大匙拌勻（圖 1），淋在炸好的豬排上。

京都汁豬排　辣醬油 1 大匙，番茄醬 1 $\frac{1}{2}$ 大匙、糖 $\frac{1}{2}$ 大匙、麻油 1 小匙水 2 大匙拌勻（圖 2），淋在炸好的豬排上。

1 Tenderize pork with a meat mallet. Mix ① with pork then marinate. Add 3 T. cornstarch to beef before deep-frying.

2 Heat oil then deep-fry pork over high heat until golden brown (about 4 minutes); remove. Serve with dipping sauce and "Shredded Chicken Salad" (see p. 92).

FIVE-FLAVORED PORK CHOPS Substitute dipping sauce with 2 T. each of soy sauce, green onions and water; 1 t. each of minced hot pepper, garlic, ginger root, sugar, sesame oil; and ½ T. vinegar (Fig. 1). Mix sauce and pour over fried pork; serve.

SWEET PORK CHOPS Substitute dipping sauce with 1 T. soy sauce, 1½ T. ketchup, ½ T. sugar, 1 t. sesame oil, and 2 T. water (Fig. 2); mix sauce and pour it over fried pork; serve.

蒜烤豬排
Roast Pork Chops & Garlic

豬大排　2 片約 8 兩（300公克）

① 醬油⋯⋯⋯⋯⋯⋯⋯3 大匙
糖、酒⋯⋯⋯⋯⋯各 1 大匙
蒜末⋯⋯⋯⋯⋯⋯½ 大匙
胡椒⋯⋯⋯⋯⋯⋯少許
檸檬⋯⋯⋯⋯⋯⋯2 片

2 pork chops, ⅔ lb. (300g)

① 3 T. soy sauce
1 T. sugar, 1 T. wine
½ T. minced garlic
dash of pepper
2 lemon slices

1 豬排用刀背略搥鬆，調①料，醃半小時以上或隔夜。

2 烤箱 500℉ 烤豬排 15 分鐘，至肉熟即可取出，上洒檸檬汁。可與「奶果番茄沙拉」（見 95 頁）共食。

☐ 如郊遊烤肉，用炭火烤，味更香美。

1 Tenderize pork with back of cleaver. Mix pork with ① and marinate at least ½ hour or overnight.

2 Roast pork at 500°F 15 minutes or until cooked; remove. Sprinkle lemon juice over pork and serve with "Avocado & Tomato Salad" (see p. 95).

☐ To add flavor, barbecue pork chops over charcoal.

葱爆小里肌
Pork Tenderloin & Green onions

豬或牛小里肌肉 8 片 ⋯⋯⋯8 兩
（300 公克）

① 醬油、太白粉⋯⋯⋯各 1 大匙
糖、蒜末⋯⋯⋯⋯各½ 大匙
酒⋯⋯⋯⋯⋯⋯⋯1 大匙
青葱（5 公分長）⋯⋯⋯1 杯

② 醬油⋯⋯⋯⋯⋯⋯2 大匙
糖⋯⋯⋯⋯⋯⋯⋯½ 大匙

8 slices of pork tenderloin, ½-inch thick, ⅔ lb. (300g)

① 1 T. each: soy sauce, cornstarch
1 T. wine
½ T. each: minced garlic, sugar
1 c. green onions, 2-inch long

② 2 T. soy sauce
½ T. sugar

1 肉片用刀背略搥鬆，調①料，醃約半小時以上。

2 油 2 大匙燒熱，中火將里肌肉煎呈金黃色肉熟（約 3 分鐘）鏟鍋邊，餘油爆香葱段，倒入②料，速翻拌起鍋。

1 Tenderize pork with back of cleaver. Mix pork with ① and marinate at least ½ hour.

2 Heat 2 T. oil. Fry pork over medium heat about 3 minutes until golden brown and cooked; move meat to side of pan. Use remaining oil to stir-fry green onions until fragrant. Add ② and mix in meat; remove immediately.

麵包粉豬排
Pork in Bread Crumbs

豬大里肌肉 2 片 …………6 兩
（ 225 公克 ）

① 酒、醬油……………… 各½大匙
鹽…… ¼ 小匙、胡椒 …… 少許

② 麵粉……………………… ¼ 杯
雞蛋（ 打散 ）……………1 個
麵包粉（ 圖 1，見 5 頁 ）…1 杯
炸油……………………… 適量
沾汁（ 見右頁 ）

2 slices pork loin,
    ½ lb. (225g)

① ½ T. each: wine, soy sauce
¼ t. salt
dash of pepper

② ¼ c. flour
1 beaten egg
1 c. bread crumbs (Fig. 1),
   (see p. 5)

oil for deep-frying
DIPPING SAUCE (see p. 57)

1️⃣ 豬肉拍鬆（ 圖 2 ），調入①料拌勻，依序沾上②料，輕壓肉面，以防炸時脫落。

2️⃣ 炸油燒中溫，放入豬排中火炸約 3 分鐘至金黃色肉熟，撈出切塊沾「沾汁」與蔬菜（ 見 88～95 頁 ）共食。

蝦、生蠔或魚排　大蝦 6 兩(225 公克)處理好（ 見 14 頁，圖 1-3 ）調酒半大匙、鹽、胡椒各少許略醃。
生蠔 6 兩(225 公克)洗淨，在沸水中煮至半熟，撈出瀝乾。
魚肉 6 兩(225 公克)切大片，沾②料炸熟，做法同上。

1️⃣ Tenderize pork with a meat mallet (Fig. 2) then mix with ① ; marinate. Coat pork with ② in the order listed then press lightly so coating will not fall off during deep-frying.

2️⃣ Heat oil to medium then deep-fry pork about 3 minutes until golden brown and cooked; remove. Cut pork into pieces; serve with vegetable (see pp. 88-95) and dipping sauce.

SHRIMP, OYSTERS, OR FISH FILLETS Prepare ½ lb. (225g) shrimp (see Figs. 1, 2, 3 on p. 14); mix in ½ T. wine, dash of pepper and salt. OR rinse ½ lb. (225g) oysters then cook in boiling water until medium rare; remove and drain. OR fillet ½ lb. (225g) fish. Coat with ② then deep-fry until cooked, procedures are the same as in above recipe.

麵包粉蔬菜
Vegetables in Bread Crumbs

① 洋葱‥‥‥‥‥‥‥‥‥‥‥ 半個
　　青椒、義大利瓜‥‥‥‥‥ 各半條
　　紅蘿蔔、地瓜‥‥‥‥‥‥ 各¼條
② 料同左頁
　　炸油‥‥‥‥‥‥‥‥‥‥ 適量
　　沾汁

① ½ onion
　　½ each: green pepper,
　　　　zucchini
　　¼ each: carrot, sweet
　　　　potato
② see ② on p. 56
　　oil for deep-frying
　　DIPPING SAUCE

■ 洋葱切圓片逐片插入牙籤固定，①料亦切片，依序沾上②料，炸至表面呈金黃色（約2分鐘），沾「沾汁」食用。

沾汁（任選一）：
Ⓐ 椒鹽（見4頁）　Ⓑ 番茄醬　Ⓒ 辣醬油　Ⓓ 海鮮醬
Ⓔ 鮮奶油沙拉醬（見8頁）　Ⓕ 鰹魚沾汁（見73頁）

■ Cut onion into rings, secure each ring with a toothpick. Slice ① . Coat vegetables with ② in the order listed; deep-fry until golden (about 2 minutes); serve with dipping sauce.

DIPPING SAUCES (choose one of the following):
Ⓐ Szechuan peppercorn salt (see p. 4)　Ⓑ Ketchup　Ⓒ Hot soy sauce
Ⓓ Hoisin sauce　Ⓔ Whipping cream salad sauce (see p. 8)
Ⓕ Bonito sauce (see p. 73)

麵包粉什錦串
Variety Kabob

　　雞肉、牛肉 ⎱
　　　　　　　 ⎰‥‥‥‥ 任選8兩
　　蝦仁、鮮貝 ⎰　　　　（300公克）
　　洋菇、鮮菇、青紅椒‥‥‥ 任選
① 酒‥‥ ½大匙、鹽‥‥ ⅓小匙
　　胡椒‥‥‥‥‥‥‥‥‥‥ 少許
　　竹籤或鐵籤（12公分長）‥8支
② 料同左頁
　　沾汁（見上）

① ⅔ lb. (300g) of any of all;
　　boned chicken, beef,
　　shelled shrimp, scallops
　　onion, mushrooms
　　green & red peppers as
　　　　desired
① ½ T. wine, ⅓ t. salt
　　dash of pepper
　　8 skewers, 5-inch long
② see ② on p.56
　　DIPPING SAUCE
　　(see above recipe)

■ 肉與蔬菜切小塊，肉調①料，串成8串，依序沾上②料；炸至表面呈金黃色肉熟（約2分鐘），沾「沾汁」食用。

■ Cut meat and vegetables into small pieces then mix with ① ; thread onto each skewer then coat with ② in the order listed. Deep-fry about 2 minutes until golden brown and cooked. Serve with dipping sauce.

甜醬肉絲
Shredded Meat & Black Beans Paste

2 人份
Serves 2

① 豬或牛里肌(切絲)·········6 兩
　　　　　　　（225 公克）
　醬油、酒、太白粉、水　各 1 大匙
② 洋葱絲、筍絲··········共 1 杯
③ 甜麵醬、醬油·······各 1 大匙
　（ 或醬油·········2 大匙 ）
　酒、糖··········各 ⅔ 大匙
　太白粉、麻油·······各 1 小匙
　水···········3 大匙

① ½ lb. (225g) shredded pork
　or beef tenderloin
　1 T. each: soy sauce, wine,
　cornstarch, water
② total of 1 c. (shredded):
　onion, bamboo shoots
③ 1 T. each: sweet bean
　paste, soy sauce (or 2 T.
　soy sauce)
　⅔ T. each: wine, sugar
　1 t. each: cornstarch,
　sesame oil
　3 T. water

1 ①料拌勻，炒前拌入油 1 大匙，炒時肉絲較易散開。

2 油 1½ 大匙燒熱，放入肉絲炒至七分熟，鏟於一邊；餘油炒香②料，隨入③料，蓋鍋見有水蒸氣冒出拌炒均勻即成。

☐ 炒好的肉絲可與荷葉餅、燒餅、生菜或其它餅皮（圖 1）包食。

☐ 任何蔬菜可選用來取代②料。

1 Mix ① . Add in 1 T. oil before frying to separate meat.

2 Heat 1½ T. oil; stir-fry meat until medium well. Move meat to side of pan. Use remaining oil to stir-fry ② until fragrant. Add ③ and mix in meat; cover and cook until steamy then stir-fry to mix well.

☐ Stir-fried pork may be served with mandarin pancakes, flaky sesame flat bread ("Shou Bing") (Fig. 1), or lettuce, etc.

☐ Other vegetables may be used to substitute ingredients ② .

魚香肉絲
Spicy Shredded Meat

① 料同左
② 辣豆瓣醬、麻油……各 $\frac{1}{2}$ 大匙
　　蔥、薑、蒜末………各 1 大匙
③ 木耳、芹菜、紅蘿蔔絲 共 1 杯
　　醬油、水…………各 2 大匙
④ 糖、酒……………各 $\frac{1}{2}$ 大匙
　　醋、太白粉…………各 1 小匙

① see ① on p. 58
② $\frac{1}{2}$ T. each: hot bean paste or chili paste, sesame oil
　1 T. each (minced): green onions, ginger root, garlic
③ total of 1 c. (shredded): wood ears, celery, carrot
④ 2 T. each: soy sauce, water
　$\frac{1}{2}$ T. each: sugar, wine
　1 t. each: vinegar, cornstarch

■ 參照左頁做法 **1**、**2**，將肉絲炒至七分熟，鏟於一邊；餘油炒香②料，隨入③料略炒，再倒入④料，蓋鍋見有水蒸氣冒出拌炒均勻即可。

□ 如有現成「魚香醬」（見 6 頁）5 大匙，可代替②、④料較簡便。

■ Follow steps **1** and **2** on p. 58 to "…Use remaining oil to stir-fry ② until fragrant." Add ③ and stir-fry briefly. Add ④ and mix in meat; cover and cook until steamy then stir-fry to mix well.

□ 5 T. spicy Hunan sauce (see p. 6) may be substituted for ingredients ② and ④.

豉椒肉絲
Shredded Meat & Black Beans

① 料同左
② 蒜、豆豉………剁碎各 1 大匙
　　蔥、薑末、麻油……各 1 小匙
③ 紅、青椒絲、洋蔥絲……共 1 杯
　　糖… $\frac{1}{2}$ 小匙、胡椒、鹽…少許
④ 酒、太白粉…………各 $\frac{1}{2}$ 大匙
　　醬油……1 大匙、水……4 大匙

① see ① on p. 58
② 1 T. each (minced): fermented black beans, garlic
　1 t. each: sesame oil, minced green onions, ginger root
③ total of 1 c. (shredded): onion, red & green peppers
④ $\frac{1}{2}$ t. sugar
　dash of pepper, salt
　$\frac{1}{2}$ T. each: wine, cornstarch
　1 T. soy sauce, 4 T. water

■ 參照左頁做法 **1**、**2**，將肉絲炒至七分熟，鏟於一邊；餘油炒香②料，隨入③料略炒，再倒入④料，蓋鍋見有水蒸氣冒出，拌炒均勻即可。

□ 如有現成「豉汁醬」（見 6 頁）5 大匙，可代替②、④料較簡便。

■ Follow steps **1** and **2** on p. 58 to "… Use remaining oil to stir-fry ② until fragrant." Add ③ and stir-fry briefly. Add ④ and mix in meat; cover and cook until steamy then stir-fry to mix well.

□ 5 T. black bean sauce (see p. 6) may be substituted for ingredients ② and ④.

碎肉生菜包
Ground Meat in Lettuce

① 牛或猪瘦絞肉 6 兩（225公克）
　　洋葱（切碎）……………… ½ 杯
② ┌ 芹菜、荸薺或筍… 切碎各 ½ 杯
　 └ 青豆仁、紅蘿蔔末…… 各 ¼ 杯
　　或冷凍綜合蔬菜丁……… 2 杯
③ ┌ 酒……………………… 1 大匙
　 │ 醬油…………………… 2 大匙
　 │ 鹽…………………… ⅓ 小匙
　 │ 糖、太白粉……… 各 1 小匙
　 │ 胡椒、麻油…………… 各少許
　 └ 水…………………… 3 大匙
　　生菜…………………… 8 片
④ 炸米粉或雲吞皮切條……… 1 杯
　　（不用亦可）

① ½ lb. (225g) ground beef
　 ½ c. chopped onion
② ┌ ½ c. each (chopped):
　 │ 　celery, water chestnuts or
　 │ 　bamboo shoots
　 │ ¼ c. each: green peas,
　 │ 　chopped carrot
　 └ or 2 c. frozen mixed
　　　vegetables
③ ┌ 1 T. wine, 2 T. soy sauce
　 │ ⅓ t. salt, 3 T. water
　 │ 1 t. each: sugar, cornstarch
　 │ dash of pepper
　 └ sesame oil as desired
　　8 lettuce leaves
④ ┌ 1 c. deep-fried rice
　 │ 　noodles or shredded
　 └ 　won ton skins (optional)

1 油 2 大匙燒熱，將①料爆炒至汁乾、油溢出時，鏟於鍋邊；再將洋葱炒香，隨入②料炒熟，最後加③料全部拌炒均勻。

2 生菜洗淨，上置炸米粉及炒熟碎肉包著吃。

□ 炸米粉時，油先燒很熱後熄火，隨入乾米粉（圖 1）炸約 5 秒鐘，脹大成 2-3 倍，撈出瀝乾油漬（圖 2）。如經常使用，可一次炸多一點，待冷封入容器內，分次使用。

1 Heat 2 T. oil; stir-fry ① until fat in meat is rendered. Move meat to side of pan; stir-fry onion until fragrant. Add ② and stir-fry until cooked. Add ③ and stir-fry to mix well.

2 Rinse lettuce then place fried rice noodles and ground meat on it; serve.

□ To deep-fry rice noodles: Heat oil until very hot. Turn off heat then deep-fry rice noodles (Fig. 1) about 5 seconds until size increases two or three times; remove and drain (Fig. 2). If fried rice noodles are used frequently, fry a large quantity then let cool and store in a container for later use.

海鮮生菜包
Seafood in Lettuce

① { 蝦、鮮貝 } ……任選 6 兩切碎
　{ 魚肉 }　　　　　（225 公克）
　洋葱（切碎）……………… ½ 杯
②、③、④料同左
　生菜………………………… 8 片

① { total of ½ lb. (225g)(diced):
　{ shrimp, scallops, fish meat
　½ c. chopped onion
②,③,④ see ②,③,④ on p. 60
　8　lettuce leaves

■ 參照左頁做法 **1**、**2**。

■ Follow steps **1** and **2** on p. 60.

碎肉豆腐
Ground Meat & Bean Curd

　牛或豬絞肉…… 4 兩（150 公克）
① { 葱末…… 2 大匙、蒜末…… 1 大匙
　{ 辣豆瓣醬………………… 1 大匙
　{ 酒……… 1 大匙、水……… ¾ 杯
② { 醬油…… 2 大匙、鹽…… ¼ 小匙
　{ 糖、麻油、胡椒………… 少許
　豆腐（切塊半盒）6兩（225公克）
③ 　太白粉、水………… 各 2 小匙
　葱花………………………… 2 大匙

　⅓ lb. (150g) ground beef or
　　pork
① { 2　T. minced green onions
　{ 1　T. minced garlic
　{ 1　T. hot bean paste
② { 2　T. soy sauce, ¼ t. salt
　{ dash of sugar, sesame oil,
　{ 　pepper
　{ 1　T. wine, ¾ c. water
　½ lb. (225g) bean curd, cut
　　into pieces
③　2　t. each: cornstarch, water
　　2　T. chopped green onions

■ 油 2 大匙燒熱，先炒香①料，隨入絞肉炒熟後，加入②料及豆腐；待滾
改小火煮約 3 分鐘，以③料勾芡成濃稠狀，撒上葱花。

□ 辣椒醬 ½ 大匙可取代辣豆瓣醬 1 大匙。

■ Heat 2 T. oil; stir-fry ① until fragrant. Add meat and stir-fry until cooked.
Add ② and bean curd then bring to boil; reduce heat to low and cook
3 minutes. Mix and add ③ to thicken; remove and sprinkle with green
onions.

□ ½ T. chili sauce may be substituted for 1 T. hot bean paste.

碎肉茄莢
Ground Meat in Eggplant

2 人份
Serves 2

長茄子…………8 兩（300 公克）
牛或豬絞肉……4 兩（150 公克）
① 醬油、水……………各 1 大匙
糖……………………………1 小匙
胡椒、麻油………………少許
太白粉…………………½ 大匙

麵糊：
水…………………………½ 杯
蛋（大）…………………1 個
麵粉………………………¾ 杯
炸油……………………適量
魚香醬或乾燒醬………4 大匙
（見 6 頁）

²/₃ lb. (300g) long eggplant
¹/₃ lb. (150g) ground beef or
   pork
1 T. each: soy sauce, water
1 t. sugar
① sesame oil as desired
   dash of pepper
¹/₂ T. cornstarch
BATTER:
¹/₂ c. water
1 large egg
³/₄ c. flour
oil for deep-frying
4 T. spicy Hunan sauce or
   spicy ketchup sauce
   (see p. 6)

1 長茄子斜切成莢狀（1 刀不切斷，1 刀切斷），約 16 片。

2 絞肉調①料拌勻。

3 打開茄莢，鑲入絞肉（圖 1）全部做好。

4 水 ½ 杯先加入蛋 1 個拌勻後，再加麵粉調勻，即為麵糊。

5 炸油燒熱，茄莢沾裹麵糊，中火炸呈金黃色至肉熟（約 4 分鐘）撈出，淋上或沾調味醬。

1 Make diagonal cut on eggplant; do not cut through. Make a second diagonal cut through eggplant to make a pocket. Follow same procedure to make about 16 pockets.

2 Mix meat with ① .

3 Open, then fill each pocket with meat (Fig. 1).

4 Mix ¹/₂ cup water with an egg. Add ³/₄ cup flour and mix well to make batter.

5 Heat oil for deep-frying. Coat meat-filled pocket with batter; deep-fry over medium heat until golden brown and cooked (about 4 minutes). Remove and serve with sauce.

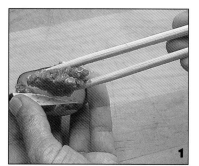

醬肉拌麵
Ground Meat & Noodles

牛或豬絞肉……6 兩（225 公克）
蒜末 1 小匙、洋葱（切碎）1 個
① 豆瓣醬……………………4 大匙
　　糖……½ 大匙、酒……2 大匙
　　麻油……1 大匙、水……½ 杯
② 洋菇、義大利瓜或黃瓜丁　4 杯
③ 太白粉……1 大匙、水……1½ 大匙
熟麵……約 12 兩（450 公克）
（見 85 頁煮麵法）

½ lb. (225g) ground beef
　　or pork
1　t. minced garlic,
1　chopped onion
① { 4　T. hot bean paste
　　½ T. sugar, 2 T. wine
　　1　T. sesame oil, ½ c. water
② { Total of 4c. (diced):
　　zucchini, mushrooms
③　1　T. cornstarch, 1½ T. water
　　1　lb. (450g) cooked dried
　　　noodles (to cook
　　　noodles, see p. 85)

■ 油 3 大匙燒熱，先炒香蒜末及洋葱，隨入絞肉炒熟後再加①料燒開；續入②料，蓋鍋煮約 2 分鐘至瓜熟，以③料勾芡成濃稠狀，澆在麵上拌食，撒上中國香菜更香。

□ 豆瓣醬可用甜麵醬、海鮮醬或醬油取代。

■ Heat 3 T. oil; stir-fry garlic and onion until fragrant. Add meat and stir-fry until cooked. Add ① and bring to boil. Add ② then cover and cook 2 minutes or until cooked. Mix and add ③ to thicken; pour over noodles and serve. Coriander may be sprinkled over meat to add flavor.

□ Sweet bean paste, hoisin sauce, or soy sauce may be substituted for hot bean paste.

碎肉煎餅
Fried Meat Patties

牛或豬絞肉……9 兩（340 公克）
　　醬油、酒………………各 1 大匙
① 鹽　¼ 小匙、胡椒、麻油　少許
　　太白粉…………………2 大匙
豆腐（壓碎）½ 杯或蛋……1 個
洋葱（切碎）………………⅓ 杯
　　蠔油或醬油……………1½ 大匙
② 糖…1 小匙、太白粉…½ 大匙
　　雞湯或水………………½ 杯

¾ lb. (340g) ground beef
　　or pork
① { 1　T. each: wine, soy sauce
　　dash of pepper
　　sesame oil as desired
　　¼ t. salt, 2 T. cornstarch
½ c. mashed bean curd
　　or 1 egg
⅓ c. chopped onion
② { 1½ T. oyster sauce
　　　or soy sauce
　　1 t. sugar, ½ T. cornstarch
　　½ c. chicken stock or water

■1 絞肉調入①料，攪拌至有黏性後，加入豆腐及洋葱再攪拌均勻，做成 8 個肉餅。

■2 油 2 大匙燒熱，先放入 4 個肉餅，蓋鍋中火煎約 2 分鐘，翻面蓋鍋續煎約 2 分鐘，至表面呈金黃色肉熟鏟出。同法再煎另 4 個肉餅。

■3 ②料煮開成薄汁澆其上，可與「燙熟生菜」（見 88 頁）配食。

■1 Mix meat with ① ; stir until sticky. Add bean curd and onion; stir until mixed well. Makes 8 meat patties.

■2 Heat 2 T. oil. Fry 4 patties over medium heat about 2 minutes; turn patties over and continue to fry 2 minutes or until golden brown and cooked. Follow the same procedures to fry the other 4 patties. Bring ② to boil then pour over patties. May be served with "Boiled Lettuce" (see p. 88).

四味龍蝦
Baked Lobster

龍蝦 1 隻 ⋯ 約 1 斤（600 公克）
調味醬⋯⋯⋯⋯⋯⋯⋯6 大匙
香菜或葱花⋯⋯⋯⋯⋯⋯2 大匙

1 lobster, 1⅓ lbs. (600g)
6 T. **SAUCE**
2 T. fresh coriander or
    chopped green onions

■ 烤箱燒至 450°F -500°F，龍蝦放入中層烤熟（約 16 分鐘），取出直切成
   兩半，趁熱淋上自己喜好的調味醬，並撒上香菜即成。

   調味醬 豉汁、宮保、魚香或乾燒等調味醬（見 6 頁）。

□ 烤熟的龍蝦可先用剪刀剪開背殼，再切成兩半較易整齊。

■ Preheat oven to 450°F-500°F; place rack in middle, bake lobster about
   16 minutes until cooked. Remove lobster and cut lengthwise in half.
   Pour sauce over lobster; sprinkle with coriander and serve.

   SAUCES (choose any of the following):
   Black bean sauce, hot spicy sauce, spicy Hunan sauce, or spicy ketchup
   sauce, etc. (see p. 6).

□ Use scissors to cut back shell open then cut lobster in half for better
   results.

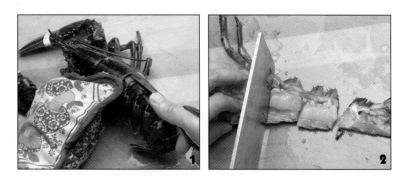

蒜烹龍蝦
Lobster & Garlic

龍蝦 1 隻 … 約 1 斤（600 公克）

① { 蒜末⋯⋯⋯⋯⋯⋯⋯⋯ 1½ 大匙
　　葱、薑末⋯⋯⋯⋯⋯ 各 1 大匙
　　酒⋯⋯⋯⋯⋯⋯⋯⋯⋯ 3 大匙

② { 鷄湯或水⋯⋯⋯⋯⋯⋯ ¾ 杯
　　鹽、糖⋯⋯⋯⋯⋯⋯ 各 ½ 小匙
　　胡椒、麻油⋯⋯⋯⋯⋯ 少許

③　太白粉…1 大匙、水…1½ 大匙
　　香菜末或葱花⋯⋯⋯⋯ 2 大匙

1　lobster, 1⅓ lbs. (600g)

① { 1½ T. minced garlic
　　1　T. each: minced green
　　　　onions, ginger root
　　3　T. wine

② { ¾ c. chicken stock or water
　　½ t. each: salt, sugar
　　dash of pepper
　　sesame oil as desired

③　1　T. cornstarch, 1½ T. water
　　2　T. minced coriander or
　　　　green onions

1 剪開龍蝦背殼（圖1）再直切半，去腸泥，由分節處切成數塊（圖2）。

2 油 2 大匙炒香①料，隨入龍蝦及酒，再加②料略翻拌後，蓋鍋小火燜煮約 5 分鐘至色變紅肉熟，加入③料勾芡成薄汁，撒上香菜末或葱花。

1 Use scissors to cut back shell open (Fig. 1) then cut lobster lengthwise in half. Devein and cut into pieces (Fig. 2).

2 Heat 2 T. oil; stir-fry ① until fragrant. Add lobster, wine, and ② then stir-fry briefly; cover and simmer 5 minutes or until shell turns red and meat is cooked. Mix and add ③ to thicken. Sprinkle with minced coriander and serve.

串燒中蝦
Shrimp Kabob

中蝦（約 20 條）8 兩（300 公克）

① { 酒⋯⋯ 1 大匙、鹽⋯⋯ ½ 小匙
　　胡椒⋯⋯⋯⋯⋯⋯⋯⋯⋯ 少許
　　長鐵籤或竹籤（15 公分）…4 支
　　檸檬⋯⋯⋯⋯⋯⋯⋯⋯⋯ ½ 個

⅔ lbs. (300g) medium
　　shrimp (about 20)

① { 1　T. wine
　　½ t. salt
　　dash of pepper
　　4　skewers, 6-inch long
　　½ lemon

1 中蝦抽去腸泥洗淨後，每 5 條蝦用一支鐵籤由中央串穿成一大排，共 4 串，依序洒上①料。

2 烤箱燒至 500°F，蝦放入中層鐵架上烤至蝦殼變紅肉熟（約 10 分鐘）。食時洒上檸檬汁味更佳。可與"蟹肉包心菜沙拉"（見 94 頁）配食。

1 Devein and rinse shrimp. Insert each skewer into the center of 5 shrimp to make 4 strings. Sprinkle with ① in the order listed.

2 Preheat oven to about 500°F. Bake shrimp at middle rack 10 minutes or until shell turns red and meat is cooked. Sprinkle with lemon juice when ready to serve. Shreds of shrimp may be served with "Crab meat & Cabbage Salad" (see p. 94).

四味大蝦片
Four Flavored Prawns

大蝦（6～8 條）8 兩（300 公克）

① 水……… 2 杯、酒 ……… 2 大匙
鹽………………………… 1 小匙
葱、薑（無亦可）…… 各 2 片

番茄黄瓜沙拉（見 92 頁）

沾汁

²/₃ lb. (300g) prawns
(about 6-8)

① 2 c. water
2 T. wine
1 t. salt
2 slices each: green onions,
ginger root (optional)

tomato and cucumber
salad (see p. 92)

DIPPING SAUCE

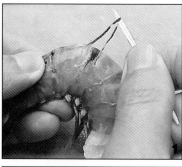

■ 蝦由背部抽出腸泥洗淨（圖 1）。①料燒開，將蝦放入煮開後改小火煮 2 分鐘熄火，續浸 2 分鐘撈出，待涼去殼，每隻片切 2～3 片，置沙拉上沾「沾汁」食用。

沾汁（任選一）：

Ⓐ 檸檬汁、醬油、白蘿蔔糊（無亦可）各 2 大匙，醋½大匙拌匀。

Ⓑ 醬油、芝麻或花生醬各 2 大匙，醋 1½ 大匙，糖⅔大匙，葱、薑、蒜、辣油或辣豆瓣醬（無亦可）各 1 小匙。

Ⓒ 醬油 4 大匙，糖、醋、麻油各½大匙，蒜末 1 大匙，辣油½大匙或辣椒醬 1 小匙（圖 2）。

Ⓓ 醬油 2 大匙，芥末醬½大匙（見 4 頁 **1**）拌匀。

■ Devein prawns (Fig. 1) and rinse. Bring ① to boil. Add prawns and bring to another boil. Reduce heat to low and continue to cook 2 minutes. Turn off heat and soak prawns 2 minutes; remove and let cool. Shell prawns; cut each prawn into 2-3 slices then place them over salad. Serve with dipping sauce.

DIPPING SAUCES (choose one of the following):

Ⓐ Mix 2 T. each of lemon juice, soy sauce, white radish paste (optional), and ½ T. vinegar.

Ⓑ Mix 2 T. each of soy sauce, sesame paste or peanut butter; 1½ T. vinegar; ²/₃ T. sugar; 1 t. each of green onions, ginger root, garlic, chili oil (or hot bean paste) (optional).

Ⓒ Mix 4 T. soy sauce; ½ T. each of sugar, vinegar, sesame oil; 1 T. minced garlic; ½ T. chili oil (or 1 t. chili paste) (Fig. 2).

Ⓓ Mix 2 T. soy sauce and ½ T. mustard sauce (see p. 4, **1**).

四味灼蝦
Four Flavored Shrimp

中蝦（約 18 條）9 兩（340 公克）

① 水⋯⋯⋯ 2 杯、酒⋯⋯⋯2 大匙
　　鹽⋯⋯⋯⋯⋯⋯⋯⋯1 小匙
　　葱、薑片（無亦可）⋯⋯各 2 片
沾汁：見左頁

3/4 lb. (340g) medium shrimp
　　(about 18)

① 2 c. water
　2 T. wine
　1 t. salt
　2 slices each: green onions,
　　ginger root (optional)
DIPPING SAUCE (see p. 66)

■ 蝦由背部抽出腸泥洗淨。①料燒開後放入蝦，待再燒開熄火續浸 2 分鐘至剛熟取出，食時去殼，沾汁食用。

■ Devein shrimp then rinse. Bring ① to boil. Add shrimp and bring to another boil. Turn off heat and soak shrimp 1-2 minutes or until cooked; remove. Shell shrimp; dip in dipping sauce when served.

爆炒蝦
Stir-fried Shrimp

中蝦（約 20 尾）9 兩（340 公克）
辣椒（曬乾或新鮮切碎）⋯⋯ 1 支
蒜末⋯⋯⋯⋯⋯⋯⋯⋯⋯1 大匙

① 酒⋯⋯3 大匙、鹽⋯⋯ 1/2 小匙
　胡椒、麻油⋯⋯⋯⋯⋯少許
葱花⋯⋯⋯⋯⋯⋯⋯⋯⋯2 大匙

3/4 lb. (340g) medium shrimp
　　(about 20)
1 dried or fresh hot pepper,
　chopped
1 T. minced garlic

① 3 T. wine, 1/2 t. salt
　sesame oil as desired
　dash of pepper
2 T. chopped green onions

1 中蝦抽出腸泥洗淨後，瀝乾水份。

2 油 2 大匙炒香辣椒、蒜末，隨入中蝦略炒，再加①料，蓋鍋用中火煮熟（約 3 分鐘見蝦顏色變紅），最後撒上葱花即成。

1 Devein shrimp; rinse and drain.

2 Heat 2 T. oil. Stir-fry hot pepper and garlic until fragrant. Add shrimp and stir-fry briefly. Add ①; cover and cook over medium heat until shrimp change color (about 3 minutes). Sprinkle with green onions and serve.

清炒蝦仁
Stir-fried Shrimp with Vegetables 2 人份
Serves 2

中蝦仁⋯⋯⋯⋯6 兩（225 公克）
① 酒⋯⋯1 大匙、鹽⋯⋯¼ 小匙
胡椒⋯ 少許、太白粉⋯¾ 大匙
炸油⋯⋯⋯⋯⋯⋯⋯⋯⋯⋯適量
木須皮⋯⋯⋯⋯⋯1 張（無亦可）
葱段（2 公分長）⋯⋯⋯⋯10 段
② 西芹、洋菇
紅蘿蔔 ⋯⋯切塊共 1 杯
③ 鹽、糖⋯⋯⋯⋯⋯⋯各⅓ 小匙
胡椒、麻油⋯⋯⋯⋯⋯各少許
太白粉⋯⋯⋯⋯⋯⋯⋯1 小匙
水⋯⋯4 大匙、酒⋯⋯½ 大匙

½ lb. (225g) medium shelled
   shrimp
① 1 T. wine, ¼ t. salt
   dash of pepper
   ¾ T. cornstarch
oil for deep-frying
1 sheet moo-shu shell
   (optional)
10 pieces green onions,
   1-inch long
② total of 1 c. (sliced): celery,
   mushrooms, carrot
③ ½ T. wine, 4 T. water
   ⅓ t. each: salt, sugar
   dash of pepper
   sesame oil as desired
   1 t. cornstarch

1 蝦仁調入①料拌勻，炒前拌入油 1 大匙，則炒時蝦仁容易分開。

2 炸油燒熱放入木須皮，用漏杓壓住中心使呈碗型（圖 1），炸至金黃色撈出（圖 2）。

3 油 1½ 大匙燒熱，放入蝦仁炒至七分熟，鏟於一邊；餘油炒香葱段，隨入②料略炒，再倒入③料，蓋鍋見有水蒸氣冒出拌炒均勻即可，盛入炸好的木須皮上。

□ 蝦的處理及炒法見 14 頁圖解。任何蔬菜可選用來取代②料。

1 Marinate shrimp in ① . To separate shrimp, add 1 T. oil and mix before frying.

2 Heat oil then deep-fry moo-shu shell. Place a hand-held strainer in center of shell and press to form a bowl shape (Fig. 1). Fry until shell is golden brown; remove (Fig. 2).

3 Heat 1½ T. oil; stir-fry shrimp until medium well. Move to side of pan; use remaining oil to stir-fry green onions until fragrant. Add ② and stir-fry briefly. Mix and add ③ ; mix in shrimp then cover and cook until steamy. Stir-fry to mix well; remove and put mixture in the fried moo-shu shell.

□ To prepare and stir-fry shrimp, see photos on p. 14. Other vegetables may be used to substitute for ingredients ② .

豉汁蝦仁
Shrimp & Black Bean Sauce

蝦仁…………6 兩（225 公克）

① 料同左

② {豆豉、蒜………剁碎各 1 大匙
　{葱、薑末、麻油……各 1 小匙

③ 青紅椒、洋葱……切塊共 1 杯

④ {醬油…… 1 大匙、水 ……5 大匙
　{鹽、胡椒… 少許、糖… ½ 小匙
　{酒、太白粉…………各 ½ 大匙

½ lb. (225g) shelled shrimp

① see ① on p. 68

② { 1 T. each (minced): garlic,
　　 fermented black beans
　{ 1 t. each: sesame oil, minced
　　 green onions, ginger root

③ total of 1 c. (cut into pieces):
　　 onion, green & red peppers

④ { 1 T. soy sauce, 5 T. water
　{ ½ t. sugar
　{ dash of pepper & salt
　{ ½ T. each: wine, cornstarch

■ 參照「清炒蝦仁」做法 **1**、**3** 將蝦仁炒至七分熟，鏟於一邊；餘油炒香② 料，隨入③料略炒，再倒入④料，蓋鍋見有水蒸氣冒出拌炒均勻即可。

□ 如有現成「豉汁醬」（見 6 頁）6 大匙，可取代②、④料較簡便。

■ Follow steps **1** and **3** on p. 68 to "... Stir-fry shrimp until medium well. Move to side of pan." Use remaining oil to stir-fry ② until fragrant. Add ③ and stir-fry briefly. Mix and add ④ ; mix in shrimp then cover and cook until steamy; stir-fry to mix well.

□ 6 T. black bean sauce (see p. 6) may be substituted for ingredients ② and ④ .

宮保蝦仁
Spicy Shrimp

蝦仁…………6 兩（225 公克）

① 料同左

② {乾辣椒(切 1 公分長去籽) 1 支
　{蒜末、麻油…………各 1 小匙

③ 腰果、洋菇…………共 1 杯

④ {醬油、水 ………各 2½ 大匙
　{糖、酒………………各 ½ 大匙
　{醋、太白粉…………各 1 小匙

½ lb. (225g) shelled shrimp

① see ① on p. 68

② { 1 dried hot pepper, cut
　　 into ½-inch long, remove
　　 seeds
　{ 1 t. each: minced garlic,
　　 sesame oil

③ { total of 1 c.: mushrooms,
　　 cashew nuts

④ { 2½ T. ea: soy sauce, water
　{ ½ T. each: sugar, wine
　{ 1 t. ea: vinegar, cornstarch

■ 參照「清炒蝦仁」做法 **1**、**3**，將蝦仁炒至七分熟，鏟於一邊；餘油炒香②料，隨入③料及④料煮開拌勻即可。

□ 如有現成「宮保醬」（見 6 頁）6 大匙，可取代②、④料較簡便。

■ Follow steps **1** and **3** on p. 68 to "... Stir-fry shrimp until medium well. Move to side of pan." Use remaining oil to stir-fry ② until fragrant. Mix ④ then add ③ and ④ ; mix in shrimp and bring to a boil. Stir-fry to mix well.

□ 6 T. hot spicy sauce (see p. 6) may be substituted for ingredients ② and ④ .

乾燒蝦仁
Shrimp & Spicy Ketchup Sauce

蝦仁…………6 兩（225 公克）

① { 酒……1 大匙、胡椒……少許
鹽…¼小匙、太白粉…¾大匙 }

② { 青葱白或洋葱（切碎）…⅓杯
蒜、薑末…………各½大匙
辣豆瓣醬或辣椒醬……1 小匙 }

③ { 番茄醬…………………3 大匙
糖、酒………………各 1 大匙
鹽…………………………¾小匙
麻油、太白粉………各½大匙
雞湯或水………………¾杯 }

½ lb. (225g) shelled shrimp

① { 1 T. wine
dash of pepper
¼ t. salt
¾ T. cornstarch }

② { ⅓ c. white part of green onions or onion, chopped
½ T. each: minced garlic, ginger root
1 t. hot bean paste or hot chili paste }

③ { 3 T. ketchup
1 T. each: sugar, wine
¾ t. salt
½ T. each: sesame oil, cornstarch
¾ c. chicken stock or water }

1 蝦仁調入①料拌勻，炒前加油 1 大匙，則炒時蝦仁易分開。

2 油1½大匙燒熱，放入蝦仁炒至七分熟，鏟於一邊；餘油炒香②料，隨入③料煮開拌勻即成。

☐ 如有現成「乾燒醬」（見 6 頁）6 大匙，可取代②、③料較簡便。

☐ 中蝦仁由背部剖開挑出腸泥（圖 1），大蝦直切半使用（圖 2）。

☐ 可用雲吞皮切條，炸呈金黃色或熟靑花菜 2 杯圍邊。

1 Marinate shrimp in ① . Add 1 T. oil before frying to separate shrimp.

2 Heat 1½ T. oil then stir-fry shrimp until medium well; move to side of pan. Use remaining oil to stir-fry ② until fragrant; mix and add ③ then bring to a boil. Stir to mix well.

☐ 6 T. spicy ketchup sauce (see p. 6) may be substituted for ingredients ② and ③ .

☐ Devein medium shrimp (Fig. 1). If large shrimp are used, cut each one in half (Fig. 2).

☐ Fried won ton strips or 2 cups cooked broccoli may be used for garnishing around the plate (optional).

辣醬蝦仁
Shrimp & Hot Paste

蝦仁‥‥‥‥‥‥6 兩（225 公克）

①、②料見左頁

③ { 小黃瓜
　　荸薺或木耳 } ‥‥‥ 切片共 1 杯

④ { 醬油、水‥‥‥‥‥各 2½ 大匙
　　糖、酒‥‥‥‥‥‥各 ½ 大匙
　　醋、太白粉‥‥‥‥各 1 小匙
　　胡椒或花椒粉‥‥‥‥‥少許

½ lb. (225g) shelled shrimp

① ② see ① , ② on p. 70

③ { total of 1 c. (sliced):gherkin
　　cucumber , water chestnuts
　　or wood ears

④ { 2½ T. each: soy sauce,water
　　½ T. each: sugar, wine
　　1 t. each: vinegar,
　　　cornstarch
　　dash of pepper or Szechuan
　　　peppercorn powder

■ 參照左頁做法 **1**、**2**，將蝦仁炒至七分熟，鏟於一邊；餘油炒香②料，隨入③料略炒，再加④料，蓋鍋見有水蒸氣冒出拌炒均勻即成。

□ 如有現成「魚香醬」（見 6 頁）6 大匙，可取代②、④料較簡便。

■ Follow steps **1** and **2** on p. 70 to "... Mix and add ③ ." Stir-fry briefly. Add ④ , mix in shrimp then cover and cook until steamy; stir-fry until mixed well.

□ 6 T. spicy Hunan sauce (see p. 6) may be substituted for ingredients ② and ④ .

蝦仁炒蛋
Shrimp & Eggs

蝦仁‥‥‥‥‥‥4 兩（150 公克）

① 料同左頁、蛋‥‥‥‥‥4 個

② { 酒‥‥ ½ 大匙、鹽‥‥ ⅓ 小匙
　　胡椒、麻油‥‥‥‥‥‥少許

任選新鮮或冷凍熟蔬菜丁 ¾ 杯

青葱花‥‥‥‥‥‥‥‥3 大匙

⅓ lb. (150g) shelled shrimp

① see ① on p. 70

4 eggs

② { ½ T. wine, ⅓ t. salt
　　dash of pepper
　　sesame oil as desired

¾ c. fresh or frozen
　vegetables, diced and
　cooked, as desired

3 T. chopped green onions

1 參照左頁做法 **1**、**2** 將蝦調味炒熟。

2 蛋先打散調②料，隨入蔬菜丁、青葱花、熟蝦仁拌勻。

3 油 3 大匙燒熱，倒入 **2** 的蝦仁等蛋汁，拌炒至蛋凝固剛熟。

1 Follow steps **1** and **2** on p. 70 to stir-fry shrimp until cooked.

2 Beat eggs. Add ② , diced vegetables, green onions, and cooked shrimp then stir-fry to mix well.

3 Heat 3 T. oil. Pour in egg mixture and stir-fry until egg is solid; remove and serve.

麵糊炸蝦
Deep-fried Shrimp

大蝦或中蝦… 12 兩（450 公克）
① { 酒……1 大匙、鹽……½ 小匙
胡椒…………………………少許
麵粉………………………6 大匙
炸油………………………適量

軟麵糊：
{ 雞蛋（打散）………………1 個
冰水……………………… ⅘ 杯
麵粉（低筋或中筋）………1 杯

或酥麵糊：
{ 冰水……………………………1 杯
麵粉（低筋或中筋）………1 杯
發粉……………………… ½ 小匙
油……………………………1 大匙
沾汁（見右頁）……………適量

1 lb. (450g) large or
medium shrimp
① { 1 T. wine, ½ t. salt
dash of pepper
6 T. flour
oil for deep-frying
SOFT BATTER:
{ 1 beaten egg
⅘ c. ice water, 1 c. flour
OR CRISPY FLOUR PASTE:
{ 1 c. ice water, 1 c. flour
½ t. baking powder, 1 T. oil
DIPPING SAUCE (see p. 73)

1 蝦去殼留尾，抽出腸泥在腹部切三刀深至一半，炸時不易捲縮（見 14 頁圖1.2），調①料，炸前沾上乾麵粉。

2 麵糊輕輕攪拌好備用。

3 炸油燒至中溫約 350°F，夾起蝦尾在麵糊內沾滾均勻下鍋，炸約 2 分鐘至外皮呈金黃色，肉熟取出置白紙上，沾「沾汁」食用。

□ 炸油溫度保持在 350°F 左右（約八分熟）炸出的效果最好。剛入材料時溫度會下降，可使用大火等溫度回升再改中火炸。

1 Shell shrimp, retain tail. Devein and make three cuts from belly to the back, do not cut through and stop half way (see Figs. 1, 2 on p. 14) so that shrimp will not curl during frying. Add ① and marinate briefly. Coat with batter or flour paste before deep-frying.

2 Stir and mix the batter well.

3 Heat oil to medium hot (about 350°F). Hold each shrimp by tail then dip in batter; deep-fry 2 minutes or until golden brown and cooked. Remove and put shrimp on a paper towel to absorb oil. Serve with dipping sauce.

□ For best results, maintain deep-frying oil at 350°F. If temperature drops when adding shrimp, increase heat until it reaches 350°F then reduce heat to maintain temperature.

麵糊魚條
Deep-fried Fish Strips

魚肉或魷魚……6 兩（225 公克）
① 料、麵糊同左頁
　炸油…………………… 適量

沾汁：同下

½ lb. (225g) fish fillet or squid
① and batter see ① and batter
　on p. 72
oil for deep-frying
DIPPING SAUCE

麵糊炸蔬菜
Deep-fried Vegetables

四季豆、洋葱、茄子
青椒、紅蘿蔔、南瓜 } …適量
地瓜、義大利瓜等
① 料、麵糊同左頁
　炸油…………………… 適量
沾汁

String beans, onion,
　eggplant, green pepper,
　carrot, squash, sweet
　potato, zucchini, etc.
　as desired
① and batter see ① and batter
　on p. 72
oil for deep-frying
DIPPING SAUCE

■ 魚肉切 5 公分長，1 公分寬長條，其餘作法同左頁 **2**、**3**。

■ Cut fish into strips, 2" x ½". Other procedures are the same as steps **2**, **3** on p. 72.

■ 四季豆切長段，其他材料切片，其餘作法同左頁 **2**、**3**。

沾汁（任選一）：
A 椒鹽（見 4 頁）。　　　　**B** 番茄醬 3 大匙。

C 鰹魚沾汁：酒 3 大匙煮開，隨入醬油 4 大匙略煮，再加水 1 杯，燒沸時加入鰹魚片 1 杯（圖 1），即刻熄火。鰹魚片全部沈底後，將汁過濾即成。食用時隨喜好添加葱花、薑末、辣椒粉、白蘿蔔糊（圖 2）等味更佳。

D 芥末調味醬：芥末醬 ½ 大匙（見 4 頁），加入醬油 2 大匙拌勻使用。

■ Cut string beans into long strips. Slice other vegetables. Other procedures are the same as steps **2** and **3** on p. 72.

　DIPPING SAUCES (choose one of the following):
A ½ T. Szechuan peppercorn salt (see p. 4).　　**B** 3 T. ketchup.

C Bonito Sauce: Bring 3 T. wine to a boil. Add 4 T. soy sauce and cook briefly. Add 1 cup water and bring to another boil. Add 1 cup dried shaved bonito (Fig. 1) and immediately turn off heat. Wait until all bonito have sunk to bottom then filter sauce. Chopped green onions, minced ginger root, hot pepper powder, daikon paste (Fig. 2), etc., may be added to enhance flavor.

D Mustard Sauce: Mix ½ T. mustard sauce (see p. 4) and 2 T. soy sauce.

五柳魚
Fish & Shredded Vegetables

魚（全魚或魚片）·約 1 斤 4 兩
（675 公克）

① 酒……………………1 大匙
　 鹽……………………1 小匙
　 胡椒…………………少許

② 青、紅椒絲
　 洋葱絲
　 香菇絲或木耳絲 ｝任選 1½ 杯
　 筍絲
　 紅蘿蔔絲

③ 醬油、糖、醋………各 3 大匙
　 水……………………½ 杯
　 太白粉………………½ 大匙
　 麻油…………………1 小匙
　 香菜…………………少許

1½ lbs. (675g) whole fish
　 or fish fillet

① 1　T. wine
　 1　t. salt
　 dash of pepper

② choose the following, as
　 desired, to total 1½ c.
　 (shredded): red & green
　 peppers, onion,
　 Chinese black mushrooms
　 (or wood ears),
　 bamboo shoots, carrot

③ 3　T. each: soy sauce, sugar,
　 vinegar
　 ½ c. water
　 ½ T. cornstarch
　 1　t. sesame oil
　 fresh coriander to taste

1 魚洗淨拭乾水份，拌入①料略醃。烤前淋油 1½ 大匙（圖 1）。

2 烤箱燒至 500℉，放入魚烤 20 分鐘至熟，取出盛盤。

3 油 2 大匙炒香②料，隨入③料煮成濃稠狀，淋於魚上；撒上香菜即成。

□ 如有現成四種口味「糖醋醬」（見 7 頁）可隨嗜好任選 1 杯取代③料。

1 Rinse fish and pat dry; marinate in ① briefly. Pour 1½ T. oil over fish before baking (Fig. 1).

2 Bake fish at 500°F until cooked, about 20 minutes.

3 Heat 2 T. oil then stir-fry ② until fragrant. Mix and add ③ ; cook until thickened. Pour mixture over fish; sprinkle with coriander and serve.

□ A cup any flavor of sweet & sour sauce (see p. 7) may be substituted for ingredients ③ .

烤魚
Baked Fish

魚⋯⋯約 1 斤 4 兩（675 公克）
① 料同左
檸檬⋯⋯⋯⋯⋯⋯⋯⋯⋯ ½個
椒鹽（見 4 頁）⋯⋯⋯ 1 小匙

1½ lbs. (675g) fish
① see ① on p. 74
½ lemon
1 t. Szechuan peppercorn
　 salt (see p. 4)

■ 參照左頁做法 **1**、**2** 烤箱燒至 500°F 放入魚烤約 20 分鐘，食用時灑上檸檬汁，沾椒鹽食用。

■ Follow steps **1** and **2** on p. 74 to bake fish. Sprinkle lemon juice over fish and serve with peppercorn salt.

茄汁淋魚
Fish & Ketchup Sauce

魚 2 片⋯⋯⋯ 12 兩（450 公克）
① 料同左
② ┌ 青蔥白或洋蔥（切碎）⋯⋯ ½杯
　├ 蒜、薑末⋯⋯⋯⋯⋯ 各 ½ 大匙
　└ 辣豆瓣醬或辣椒醬⋯⋯⋯ 1 小匙
③ ┌ 番茄醬⋯ 3 大匙、鹽⋯ ½ 小匙
　│ 酒、糖⋯⋯⋯⋯⋯⋯ 各 1 大匙
　│ 麻油、太白粉⋯⋯⋯ 各 ½ 大匙
　└ 雞湯或水⋯⋯⋯⋯⋯⋯⋯ ¾杯

2 slices of fish, 1 lb. (450g)
① see ① on p. 74
② ┌ ½ c. chopped white part of
　│ 　green onions or onion
　│ ½ T. each: minced garlic,
　│ 　ginger root
　└ 1 t. hot bean paste or hot
　 　chili paste
③ ┌ 3 T. ketchup, ½ t. salt
　│ 1 T. each: wine, sugar
　│ ½ T. each: sesame oil,
　│ 　cornstarch
　└ ¾ c. stock or water

1 參照左頁做法 **1**、**2**，烤箱燒至 500°F 放入魚烤約 15 分鐘。

2 油 3 大匙炒香②料，隨入③料煮成濃稠狀，淋在烤好的魚上即成。

□ 如有現成乾燒醬（見 6 頁）1 杯，可取代②、③料較簡便。

1 Follow steps **1** and **2** on p. 74 to bake fish at 500°F 15 minutes.

2 Heat 3 T. oil and stir-fry ② until fragrant. Mix and add ③; cook until thickened. Pour over baked fish.

□ A cup spicy ketchup sauce (see p. 6) may be substituted for ingredients ② and ③.

清蒸魚
Steamed Fish

魚……………1 斤（600 公克）
① 酒……………………1 大匙
　 鹽……………………½ 小匙
② 葱（切絲）……………¼ 杯
　 新鮮辣椒或紅蘿蔔絲……1 大匙
　 胡椒…………………少許
　 麻油…………………1 小匙
醬油…………………2½ 大匙
香菜…………………少許

1⅓ lbs. (600g) fish

① { 1　T. wine
　 { ½ t. salt

② { ¼ c. shredded green onions
　 { 1　T. shredded fresh hot
　 　　　pepper or carrot
　 dash of pepper
　 { 1　t. sesame oil
2½ T. soy sauce
fresh coriander to taste

■ 魚處理乾淨（見 15 頁）拭乾水份，灑上①料略醃，置於蒸盤內，水開大火蒸約 12 分鐘（魚排約 8 分鐘），倒出餘汁；撒上②料，淋上燒滾熱油 2 大匙及醬油、香菜即成。

□ 用微波爐需 5～8 分鐘。

□ 任何新鮮魚類均可使用，蒸的時間視魚的厚度不同。

■ Prepare fish (see p. 15) then pat dry; marinate in ① briefly. Bring water to boil; steam fish at high about 12 minutes. (If fish fillet is used, steam 8 minutes.) Remove and discard liquid. Sprinkle fish with ② then pour 2 T. hot boiling oil over it. Add soy sauce and coriander; serve.

□ Fish may be cooked in microwave at high 5-8 minutes.

□ Any kind of fresh fish may be used for this dish. Adjust steaming time according to thickness of fish.

辣醬淋魚
Fish & Hot
Bean Paste

魚排（淨肉）‥‥‥9 兩（340 公克）

① 料同左

②{ 辣豆瓣醬或辣椒醬‥‥‥‥½大匙
　 蔥、薑、蒜末‥‥‥‥‥各 1 大匙
　 麻油‥‥‥‥‥‥‥‥‥‥½大匙

青蔥花‥‥‥‥‥‥‥‥‥3 大匙

③{ 酒、醬油‥‥‥‥‥‥各 3 大匙
　 醋、糖、太白粉‥‥‥各 ½大匙
　 水‥‥‥6 大匙、胡椒‥‥少許

¾ lb. (340g) fish fillet

① see ① on p. 76

②{ ½ T. hot bean paste or hot
　　chili paste
　　1 T. each (minced): green
　　onions, ginger root, garlic
　　½ T. sesame oil

　　3 T. chopped green onions

③{ 3 T. each: wine, soy sauce
　　½ T. each: vinegar, sugar
　　½ T. cornstarch
　　6 T. water, dash of pepper

1 油 2 大匙炒香②料，隨入③料煮開成濃稠狀。

2 魚排灑上①料（圖 1 ），烤箱燒至 500°F 烤約 15 分鐘至熟，淋上做好的調味醬，撒上蔥花即成。

☐ 如有現成「魚香醬」（見 6 頁）½杯，可取代②、③料較簡便。

1 Heat 2 T. oil then stir-fry ② until fragrant. Mix and add ③ ; cook until thickened.

2 Sprinkle ① over fish (Fig. 1). Preheat oven to 500°F then bake fish until cooked (about 15 minutes). Pour sauce over fish and sprinkle with green onions. Serve.

☐ ½ cup spicy Hunan sauce (see p. 6) may be substituted for ingredients ② and ③ .

香醋淋魚
Fish & Vinegar

魚排（切塊圖 2 ）‥‥‥‥‥9 兩
　　　　　　　　　　（340 公克）

① 料同左

②{ 醬油‥‥3 大匙、黑醋‥‥1 大匙
　 麻油、糖、蒜、薑末 各 ½大匙
　 蔥花‥‥2 大匙、辣椒片‥‥適量

¾ lb. (340g) fish, cut into
　pieces (Fig. 2)

① see ① on p. 76

②{ 3 T. soy sauce
　　1 T. black vinegar
　　½ T. each: sesame oil, sugar,
　　　minced garlic, ginger root
　　2 T. chopped green onions
　　1 hot pepper, sliced

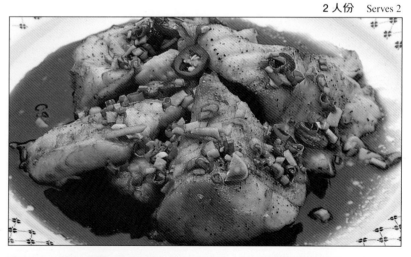

■ 參照上面做法 **2**，將魚烤約 15 分鐘至熟。淋上拌好的②料即成。

☐ 魚表面沾上少許太白粉或麵粉，煎或炸熟後淋汁非常可口。

■ Follow step **2** in above recipe to bake fish; mix and pour ② over fish. Serve.

☐ Fish may also be fried or deep-fried after coating with cornstarch (or flour); then pour on sauce.

薑葱炒蟹
Stir-fried Crab

蟹…………1 斤半（900 公克）
葱段……………………1 杯
（切7 公分長葱白、葱葉分開）
薑片…………………………6 片
酒………………………………3 大匙
① { 醬油…………………………1 大匙
蠔油或醬油…………………1 大匙
胡椒、麻油……………………少許
雞湯或水………………………¾ 杯
② { 太白粉………………………⅔ 大匙
水……………………………1 大匙

2 lbs. (900g) crab
1 c. green onion sections
    (3-inch long), separate
    green & white parts
6 slices ginger root
3 T. wine
① { 1 T. soy sauce
dash of pepper
1 T. oyster sauce or soy
    sauce
sesame oil as desired
¾ c. chicken stock or water
② { ⅔ T. cornstarch
1 T. water

1 蟹處理乾淨切塊（見 15 頁）。

2 油 2 大匙燒熱，先炒香葱白及薑片，隨入蟹塊及酒略炒，續入①料，蓋鍋用中火燒煮約 5 分鐘，至汁剩約一半蟹肉熟時，加入葱葉，用②料勾成薄汁，即可盛盤。

1 Prepare crab and cut into pieces (see p. 15).

2 Heat 2 T. oil; stir-fry white part of green onions and ginger root until fragrant. Add crab and wine then stir-fry briefly. Add ① ; cover and cook over medium heat 5 minutes or until liquid is reduced to half and crab is cooked. Mix and add ② to thicken; remove and serve.

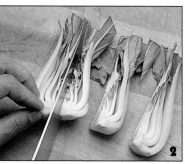

豉汁炒蟹
Crab & Black
Bean Sauce

蟹…………1 斤半（900 公克）

① 豆豉（切碎）…………2 大匙
葱、薑、蒜末………各 ½ 大匙

② 醬油…1½ 大匙、鹽…¼ 小匙
糖 1 小匙、胡椒、麻油 少許
酒……3 大匙、水………½ 杯
太白粉…………………½ 大匙

洋葱、青、紅椒(切塊)各 ½ 杯

2 lbs. (900g) crab

① 2 T. fermented black beans, minced
½ T. each (minced): green onions, garlic, ginger root

② 1½ T. soy sauce, ¼ t. salt,
1 t. sugar, dash of pepper
sesame oil as desired
3 T. wine, ½ c. water
½ T. cornstarch

½ c. each (sliced): onion, green & red peppers

1 蟹處理乾淨切塊（見 15 頁）。

2 油 2 大匙炒香①料，隨入蟹塊略炒後加入②料，蓋鍋煮 5 分鐘，再加洋葱、青、紅椒，蓋鍋煮至水蒸氣冒出，蟹肉熟，汁成濃稠狀即成。

☐ 如有現成「豉汁醬」（見 6 頁）½ 杯加水 ½ 杯，可取代①、②料。

1 Prepare crab and cut into pieces (see p. 15).

2 Heat 2 T. oil then stir-fry ① until fragrant. Add crab and stir-fry briefly. Mix and add ② ; cover and cook 5 minutes. Add onion, green & red peppers; cover and cook until crab is cooked and liquid thickens and steams. Remove and serve.

☐ ½ cup black bean sauce (see p. 6) and ½ cup water may be substituted for ① and ② .

蟹肉靑梗菜
Crab & Bok
Choy

靑梗菜或靑花菜…………12 兩
　　　　　　　　　（450 公克）

葱段（3 公分長）…………6 段

① 酒……1 大匙、鹽……½ 小匙
胡椒、麻油………………少許
鷄湯或水…………………1 杯

蟹肉（圖 1）…………………½ 杯

② 太白粉…1 大匙、水…1½ 大匙

1 lb. (450g) bok choy or broccoli

6 sections green onions, 1-inch long

① 1 T. wine, ½ t. salt
dash of pepper
sesame oil as desired
1 c. chicken stock or water

½ c. crab meat (Fig. 1)

② 1 T. cornstarch
1½ T. water

1 靑梗菜選大小整齊去老葉，每棵切開成四瓣（圖 2）洗淨待用。

2 油 2 大匙炒香葱段，隨入①料燒開後續入靑梗菜，蓋鍋煮約 2 分鐘，加入蟹肉續煮 1 分鐘，用②料勾芡，將靑梗菜排於四周，蟹肉置中央可增美感。

1 Choose the same size bok choy and remove wilted leaves. Cut each bok choy into fourths (Fig. 2); rinse and set aside.

2 Heat 2 T. oil; stir-fry green onions until fragrant. Add ① and bring to a boil. Add bok choy; cover and cook about 2 minutes. Add crab and continue to cook 1 minute. Mix and add ② to thicken. Arrange bok choy around plate then place crab in center.

蟹肉炒蛋
Stir-fried Crab & Eggs

2 人份
Serves 2

蟹肉（或熟蝦仁）………… ½ 杯

① { 洋蔥絲
紅蘿蔔絲
香菇絲或洋菇片 } …… 各 ¼ 杯

② { 蛋………………………… 3 個
鹽、糖………………… 各 ⅓ 小匙
胡椒、麻油…………………… 少許

③ { 雞湯或水…………………… ¾ 杯
番茄醬………………… 1 ½ 大匙
糖、太白粉………… 各 1 小匙
鹽…………………………… ¼ 小匙

½ c. crab meat or cooked
    shelled shrimp

① { ¼ c. each: shredded onion,
carrot, Chinese black
mushrooms (or sliced
mushrooms)

② { 3 eggs
sesame oil as desired
⅓ t. each: salt, sugar
dash of pepper

③ { ¾ c. chicken stock or water
1½ T. ketchup
1 t. each: sugar, cornstarch
¼ t. salt

1 蟹肉與①料、②料全部拌勻。

2 油 3 大匙燒熱，先輕搖一下使油均勻遍佈鍋面，倒入拌好的蛋，中火炒至蛋剛熟，鏟出放入中碗內 1 分鐘，倒扣於盤內，使蛋呈半球型。

3 ③料煮開成薄糊狀，淋在炒蛋上即成。

☐ ③料內可酌加青椒絲、紅蘿蔔絲、洋菇片或香菇絲同煮，澆淋在蛋上加以變化。

1 Mix crab meat, ① , and ② well.

2 Heat 3 T. oil then shake pan lightly to distribute oil evenly. Pour in egg mixture and stir-fry over medium heat until just cooked. Remove and put in a medium bowl 1 minute. Place a plate upside down, on the bowl; hold plate against bowl and turn them over to put egg mixture onto the plate.

3 Bring ③ to boil then cook until thickened; pour over the egg and serve.

☐ Shredded green pepper, carrot, Chinese black mushrooms or sliced mushrooms may be cooked with ③ then poured over eggs.

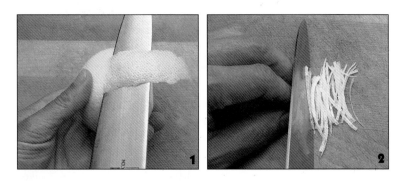

海鮮蒸蛋
Steamed Eggs & Seafood

① { 蝦仁、魚、蟹肉、
蛤蜊、生蠔、鮮貝 } 任選 ⅔ 杯

蛋……………………2 個

② { 鹽……⅔ 小匙、麻油……½ 小匙
酒……½ 大匙、水……1⅓ 杯

香菜…………………少許

檸檬黃色表皮（切絲）…少許

① { choose the following, as desired, to total ⅔ c.: shelled shrimp, fish meat, clams, crab meat, oysters, scallops

2 eggs

② { 1⅓ c. water, ⅔ t. salt
½ t. sesame oil, ½ T. wine

fresh coriander as desired

shredded lemon skin as desired

■ 蛋先打散後拌入②料，倒入蒸碗或分盛兩碗，再加入①料；水開小火蒸約 15 分鐘至蛋剛凝固（用竹籤插入無蛋汁流出或不粘），撒上香菜或檸檬皮絲（圖 1.2）味更香。

□ 用微波爐需 6～8 分鐘。

■ Beat eggs then add ② ; stir and pour into two bowls. Add ① and steam egg mixture over low heat 15 minutes or until eggs become solid; test the doneness by inserting a toothpick. Coriander or shredded lemon peel (Figs. 1, 2) may be sprinkled over the steamed eggs to add flavor.

□ If microwave is used, cook at high 6-8 minutes.

炒海瓜子
Stir-fried Clams

海瓜子…………1 斤(600 公克)

① { 蒜末……1 大匙、薑末……½ 大匙
新鮮或乾辣椒（切碎）……1 大匙

② { 酒……3 大匙、鹽……¼ 小匙
胡椒、麻油………………少許

③ { 太白粉…………………1 小匙
水………………………1 大匙

1⅓ lbs. (600g) clams

① { 1 T. minced garlic
½ T. minced ginger root
1 T. chopped fresh or dried hot pepper

② { 3 T. wine, ¼ t. salt
dash of pepper
sesame oil as desired

③ { 1 t. cornstarch
1 T. water

1 海瓜子洗淨，瀝乾水份。

2 油 2 大匙炒香①料，隨入海瓜子用大火略炒後，倒入②料；蓋鍋見水蒸氣冒出，見殼打開肉熟時，用③料勾成薄汁。可與熟麵拌食。

豉汁炒蜆 如有現成「豉汁醬」（見 6 頁）6 大匙，可取代①、②、③ 料。洋蔥、青椒片加入同炒更佳。

1 Rinse clams then drain.

2 Heat 2 T. oil then stir-fry ①. Add clams and stir-fry briefly over high heat. Add ② ; cover and cook until steamy and clam shells open. Mix and add ③ to thicken; remove and serve with cooked noodles.

CLAMS WITH BLACK BEAN SAUCE substitute 6 T. black bean sauce (see p. 6) for ingredients ① , ② , and ③ . Sliced onion and green pepper may be added for extra flavor.

魷魚雙樣
Baked Squid & Dipping Sauce

2 人份
Serves 2

魷或墨魚（淨肉）8 兩（300 公克）

① { 酒1大匙、鹽 ¼ 小匙、胡椒少許
黑或白芝麻（如無亦可）½ 大匙

沾汁：

Ⓐ { 醬油、檸檬汁……… 各 2 大匙
醋……………………… ⅔ 大匙

或

Ⓑ { 醬油…………………… 3 大匙
糖、醋、辣油……… 各 ½ 大匙
蒜泥、麻油………… 各 ⅔ 大匙

或

Ⓒ { 番茄醬‥2 大匙、醬油‥1 大匙
蔥、薑、蒜末……… 各 ½ 大匙
麻油、糖、醋……… 各 1 小匙

⅔ lb. (300g) squid or
cuttlefish (net weight)

① { 1 T. wine, ¼ t. salt
dash of pepper
½ T. black or white sesame
seeds (optional)

DIPPING SAUCE:

Ⓐ { 2 T. each: soy sauce,
lemon juice
⅔ T. vinegar

OR

Ⓑ { 3 T. soy sauce
½ T. each: sugar, vinegar,
chili oil
⅔ T. each: minced garlic,
sesame oil

OR

Ⓒ { 2 T. ketchup, 1 T. soy sauce
½ T. each: minced green
onions, ginger root, garlic
1 t. each: sesame oil, sugar,
vinegar

■ 魷魚處理乾淨（見 15 頁），拭乾水份，在內面劃交叉刀痕（圖 1），依序洒上①料，表皮面朝下鋪在烤網上。烤箱燒至 500°F，魷魚置中層，烤約 10 分鐘；至表面呈金黃色肉熟，切塊置盤，沾「沾汁」食用。

□ 如用水煮，在滾水內中火川燙約 2 分鐘至剛熟，撈出瀝乾水份。切塊沾「沾汁」食用。

□ 魷魚或墨魚市場有處理乾淨的冷凍品出售（圖 2）使用方便。

■ Prepare squid (see p. 15) then pat dry. Make diagonal cuts to ⅔ deep on the inside surface of the squid; turn over and make cross diagonal cuts to ⅔ deep to form diamond-shape cuts (Fig. 1). Sprinkle with ① in order listed then put squid on a baking pan, skin side down. Preheat oven to 500°F; put pan on middle rack and bake until golden brown and cooked (about 10 minutes). Cut squid into pieces then serve with any desired dipping sauce listed above.

□ Squid may be cooked over medium heat in boiling water about 2 minutes then removed, drained, and served with any desired dipping sauce.

□ Frozen and processed squid or cuttlefish (Fig. 2) may be used for convenience.

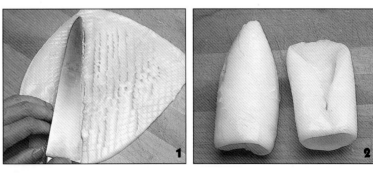

清炒墨魚
Stir-fried Cuttlefish

魷或墨魚(淨肉)8 兩(300 公克)

①
- 酒……1 大匙、鹽……$\frac{1}{6}$ 小匙
- 太白粉…………………1 大匙
- 蒜、薑末…………… 各 $\frac{1}{2}$ 大匙
- 任選蔬菜（切片）…… $1\frac{1}{2}$ 杯

②
- 鹽、糖‥各 $\frac{1}{3}$ 小匙、酒‥1 大匙
- 胡椒、麻油…………………少許
- 太白粉…………………$\frac{1}{2}$ 大匙
- 鷄湯或水………………6 大匙

$\frac{2}{3}$ lb. (300g) squid or cuttlefish (net weight)

①
- 1 T. wine, $\frac{1}{6}$ t. salt
- 1 T. cornstarch
- $\frac{1}{2}$ T. each: minced garlic, ginger root
- $1\frac{1}{2}$ c. mixed vegetables, sliced

②
- $\frac{1}{3}$ t. each: salt, sugar
- dash of pepper
- sesame oil as desired
- 1 T. wine, $\frac{1}{2}$ T. cornstarch
- 6 T. chicken stock or water

1 魷魚或墨魚處理乾淨切塊（見 15 頁），調入①料拌勻略醃。

2 2 大匙油燒熱，放入魷魚片炒至捲起取出；餘油先炒香蒜、薑末，隨入蔬菜略炒，最後加入②料及魷魚，蓋鍋見水蒸氣冒出拌炒均勻即成。

1 Prepare cuttlefish then cut into pieces (p. 15); mix in ① and marinate briefly.

2 Heat 2 T. oil then stir-fry squid until it curls; remove squid. Use remaining oil to stir-fry garlic and ginger root until fragrant. Add vegetables and stir-fry briefly. Add ② and cuttlefish; cover and cook until steamy then stir-fry to mix well. Serve.

宮保鮮魷
Spicy Squid

魷或墨魚(淨肉)8 兩(300 公克)

① 料同上

②
- 乾辣椒(切 1 公分長去籽) 1 支
- 蒜末…1 小匙、麻油… $\frac{1}{2}$ 大匙
- 任選蔬菜（切塊）…………1 杯

③
- 醬油、水…………… 各 $2\frac{1}{2}$ 大匙
- 糖、酒……………… 各 $\frac{1}{2}$ 大匙
- 醋、太白粉………… 各 1 小匙

$\frac{2}{3}$ lb. (300g) squid or cuttlefish (net weight)

① see ① in above recipe

②
- 1 dried hot pepper, cut $\frac{1}{2}$-inch long
- 1 t. minced garlic
- $\frac{1}{2}$ T. sesame oil
- 1 c. mixed vegetables, cut into pieces

③
- $2\frac{1}{2}$ T. each: soy sauce, water
- $\frac{1}{2}$ T. each: sugar, wine
- 1 t. each: vinegar, cornstarch

■ 參照清炒墨魚做法 **1**、**2** 將魷魚炒熟取出，餘油炒香②料，隨入蔬菜略炒，續加③料及魷魚，蓋鍋見水蒸氣冒出拌炒均勻即成。

□ 如有現成宮保醬（見 6 頁）6 大匙，可取代②、③料較簡便。

■ Follow steps **1** and **2** in above recipe to stir-fry squid. Use remaining oil to stir-fry ② until fragrant. Add vegetables and stir-fry briefly. Add ③ and squid; cover and cook until steamy then stir-fry to mix well.

□ 6 T. hot spicy sauce (see p. 6) may be substituted for ingredients ② and ③.

炒飯
Fried Rice

2 人份
Serves 2

飯⋯⋯⋯⋯⋯⋯⋯⋯3 杯
蛋（打勻）⋯⋯⋯⋯⋯2 個
葱或洋葱末⋯⋯⋯⋯⋯3 大匙
蝦仁、火腿
香腸或絞肉 ⎫ 4 兩（150 公克）

① 任選蔬菜切丁⋯⋯⋯⋯ 共 1 杯
② ⎰ 鹽、糖⋯⋯⋯⋯⋯⋯½ 小匙
　 ⎱ 醬油⋯ 1 大匙、胡椒⋯ 少許

3　c. cooked rice
2　eggs, beaten
3　T. minced green onions
　　or onion
⅓　lb. (150g) shelled shrimp,
　　ham, sausage or ground
　　meat
①　1 c. mixed vegetables, diced
②　⎰ ½ t. each: salt, sugar
　　⎱ 1 T. soy sauce
　　　dash of pepper

■ 油 4 大匙燒熱，先將蛋炒熟，隨入葱炒香，再加蝦仁炒熟後，續入①
料、飯及②料，全部拌炒至飯熱材料均勻（約 3 分鐘）。

□ ①料的蔬菜可使用冷凍綜合蔬菜。

煮飯法　1½ 杯米用水多次冲洗瀝乾，再加水 1½ 杯，浸泡 ½～1 小時。先
用大火燒開 1 分鐘，蓋鍋改小火續煮 20 分鐘，熄火再燜 10 分鐘。或用
電鍋更方便。

燴飯　炒雞丁（見 32～35 頁）、紅燒或炒牛肉（見 42-43 頁及 48-51 頁）、
炒肉絲（見 58～59 頁）或炒蝦仁（見 68-69 頁），任選一種加在飯上即成。

■ Heat 4 T. oil then stir-fry eggs until cooked. Add green onions and stir-
fry until fragrant; add shrimp and stir-fry until cooked. Add ① , rice, and
② ; stir-fry until rice is hot and all ingredients are mixed well, about 3
minutes.

□ Frozen, mixed vegetables may be substituted for ingredients ① .

TO COOK RICE　Rinse 1½ cups rice several times then drain. Add 1½ cups
water and soak the rice in water ½ to 1 hour then cook over high heat
1 minute; cover, reduce heat to low and continue to cook 20 minutes.
Turn off heat and wait 10 minutes; serve. A rice cooker may be used for
convenience.

FOOD OVER RICE　Choose any of the following: Stir-fried chicken (see
pp. 32-35), beef in sauces or stir-fried beef (see pp. 42-43, 48-51), stir-
fried meat (see pp. 58-59), or stir-fried shrimp (see pp. 68-69). Pour
food over the rice and serve.

炒麵
Fried Noodles

乾麵(煮熟)‥‥‥‥4 兩(150 公克)
肉絲‥‥‥‥‥‥‥4 兩(150 公克)
葱‥‥‥‥‥‥‥‥‥‥‥8 小段
醬油‥‥‥‥‥‥‥‥‥‥1 大匙

① { 包心菜、紅蘿蔔絲
　　豆芽菜 } ‥‥共 3 杯

② { 酒、醋‥‥‥‥‥‥各 $\frac{1}{2}$ 大匙
　　鹽、糖、辣椒醬‥‥各 $\frac{1}{2}$ 小匙
　　胡椒、麻油‥‥‥‥‥‥少許
　　雞湯或水‥‥‥‥‥‥$\frac{1}{3}$ 杯

$^1/_3$ lb. (150g) dried noodles
$^1/_3$ lb. (150g) shredded meat
8　sections of green onions,
　　1-inch long
1　T. soy sauce

① { total of 3 c.: bean sprouts,
　　　shredded cabbage, carrot

② { $^1/_2$ T. each: wine, vinegar
　　$^1/_2$ t. each: salt, sugar, hot
　　　chili paste
　　dash of pepper
　　sesame oil as desired
　　$^1/_3$ c. chicken stock or water

燴麵
Food Over
Noodles

乾麵‥‥‥‥‥‥‥4 兩(150 公克)
或生麵‥‥‥‥‥‥6 兩(225 公克)
（ 煮熟後為 12 兩熟麵 ）

$^1/_3$ lb. (150g) dried noodles
　or $^1/_2$ lb. (225g) fresh
　noodles
($^1/_3$ lb. dried noodles can
　make 1 lb. cooked
　noodles)

■　油 3 大匙燒熱，炒香葱段，隨入肉絲炒熟，再加醬油 1 大匙略炒後，續入①、②料，將蔬菜炒熟後，加入熟麵條拌炒約 2 分鐘。

□　肉可選雞、豬、牛、或火腿。蔬菜如菠菜、韮菜、香菇、筍等均可使用。

■　Cook noodles (see recipe below). Heat 3 T. oil then stir-fry green onions until fragrant. Add meat and stir-fry until cooked; add 1 T. soy sauce and stir-fry briefly. Add ① and ② ; stir-fry until vegetables are cooked. Add noodles and stir-fry to mix well, about 2 minutes. Serve.

□　Meat such as chicken, pork, beef, or ham; and vegetables, such as spinach, Chinese leek, Chinese black mushrooms, bamboo shoots, etc., may be used in this recipe.

■　參照左頁燴飯，任選一種菜淋在熟麵上即成。亦可將熟麵兩面煎黃或用烤箱 500 ℉烤約 8 分鐘再淋上燴麵材料。

煮麵法　半鍋水燒開、入麵條輕攪拌、大火燒開，視麵的種類，將麵煮熟，撈出瀝乾，拌油 1 大匙。

■　Choose any food listed in "Food Over Rice" (see P. 84) and pour over cooked noodles. OR cooked noodles may be fried until both sides are golden, or baked at 500°F about 8 minutes then pour food over noodles and serve.

TO COOK NOODLES　Bring half pot of water to boil; add noodles and stir. Bring water to another boil; reduce heat to medium and cook about 5 minutes. Remove and drain noodles then mix with 1 T. oil.

粟米羹
Corn Soup

① { 粟米醬·················1 罐
　 雞湯或水·····4 杯、酒·····1 大匙
　 鹽······ 1 小匙、胡椒 ····· 少許 }

② { 蝦仁、蟹肉、魚肉
　 貝類、絞肉、火腿 } 任選半杯

③ { 太白粉·················· 2½ 大匙
　 水··················3 大匙 }
　 蛋（打勻）·················1 個

① {
1　can creamed corn
4　c. chicken stock or water
1　T. wine
1　t. salt
dash of pepper
}

② {
choose one or several of
　the following to total ½ c.:
　shelled shrimp, crab meat,
　fish meat, scallops,
　ground meat, ham
}

③ {
2½ T. cornstarch
3　T. water
}
1　egg, beaten

■ ①料燒開，加②料再燒開，用③料勾芡成薄糊狀；改小火再將蛋汁徐徐加入，邊攪拌至蛋熟即可。

□ 粟米罐有顆粒狀和攪碎糊狀，可單獨或混合使用。

高湯　鍋內放入雞、牛或豬的肉或骨並加水（比例約為 1：4）燒開，取出泡沫及油漬加少許酒、葱、薑片，改小火煮約 1～3 小時即成美味高湯。如趁熱裝入真空容器或冷凍，可保長時間不壞。也可買現成雞湯使用。

■ Bring ① to boil; add ② and bring to another boil. Mix and add ③ to thicken. Reduce heat to low; gradually pour egg into soup and stir until egg is cooked. Remove and serve.

□ There are two kinds of canned corn - whole kernel and cream style corn; they can be mixed or used separately.

STOCK　Put meat or bone of chicken, beef or pork in a pot then add water at a ratio of 1:4; bring water to boil then remove bubbles and grease on the top. Add some wine, green onions, and ginger root slices then reduce heat to low and cook 1-3 hours. Chicken stock is very useful in cooking home style meals. The stock can last for a long time without spoiling if it is stored in an air-tight container immediately while it is hot. Ready-made chicken broth may also be used for convenience.

蔬菜肉片湯
Vegetables & Meat Soup

①　鶏、豬、或牛肉片………½ 杯
①　{ 鹽…………………………⅛ 小匙
　　{ 太白粉……………………1 小匙
②　{ 鹽……………………………1 小匙
　　{ 酒………………………………½ 大匙
　　{ 胡椒、麻油………………少許
　　{ 鶏湯…………………………4 杯
　　任選蔬菜切片…………共 1 杯

½ c. sliced chicken, pork,
　　or beef

① { ⅛ t. salt
　 { 1　t. cornstarch

② { 1　t. salt
　 { ½ T. wine
　 { sesame oil as desired
　 { dash of pepper
　 { 4　c. chicken stock
　 1　c. mixed vegetables,
　　　sliced

■ 肉調①料拌勻。②料燒開，隨入肉及蔬菜煮熟即成。

□ 肉與蔬菜切法一致（如肉切片時，蔬菜也切片）較爲美觀。

■ Add ① to meat; stir to mix well. Bring ② to boil; add meat and vegetables and cook until all ingredients are cooked.

□ If meat is sliced, slice vegetables to have uniformity and a more
appealing presentation.

豆腐蛋花羹
Bean Curd & Egg Soup

①　鶏、豬、牛肉或火腿絲…… ½ 杯
①　醬油 ½ 大匙、太白粉……1 小匙
②　{ 鹽 ⅓ 小匙、胡椒、麻油 少許
　　{ 醬油……2 大匙、雞湯……4 杯
　　蔬菜任選、豆腐……切絲各 1 杯
③　太白粉……3 大匙、水……4 大匙
　　蛋（打勻）………………2 個

½ c. sliced chicken, pork,
　　beef, or ham

① { ½ T. soy sauce
　 { 1 t. cornstarch

② { ⅓ t. salt, 2 T. soy sauce
　 { dash of pepper
　 { sesame oil as desired
　 { 4　c. chicken stock
　 1　c. mixed vegetables,
　　　shredded
　 1　c. bean curd, cut into
　　　strips

③ 3　T. cornstarch, 4 T. water
　 2　eggs, beaten

■ 肉絲調①料拌勻，②料燒開後放入肉絲拌開，隨入蔬菜及豆腐再煮開，以
③料勾成濃汁，即可徐徐加入蛋汁，蛋花浮起即熄火。

酸辣湯　將做好的豆腐蛋花羹加入醋 2 大匙、胡椒 ⅓ 小匙拌勻即成。

■ Add ① to the meat; stir to mix well. Bring ② to a boil; add meat and stir
to separate. Add vegetables and bean curd; bring to another boil. Mix
and add ③ to thicken. Gradually pour eggs into the soup; stir until eggs
float. Remove and serve.

HOT & SOUR SOUP　Add 2 T. vinegar and ⅓ t. black pepper to soup; stir
to mix well and serve.

簡易燙熟蔬菜
Easy Boiled Vegetables

蔬菜………… 8 兩（300 公克）
川燙用料：
① 水………6 杯、鹽…… 1 小匙
沙拉油………………… 2 大匙

② ⅔ lb. (300g) vegetables
for cooking vegetables:
① 6 c. water
1 t. salt
2 T. oil

靑花菜、義大利瓜 Broccoli & Zucchini

■ 靑花菜分切小朵洗淨，莖部去除老皮，切片。義大利瓜（或去皮絲瓜）切除兩端硬部切片。①料煮開，入靑花菜和義大利瓜燙 2 分鐘，取出淋沾汁。

■ Separate broccoli into flowerets and rinse. Remove hard skin from stem then slice stem. Cut off both ends of zucchini (or skinless sponge-gourd) then slice. Bring ① to boil; cook broccoli and zucchini for 2 minutes. Remove vegetables and serve with seasoning.

芥蘭菜 Chinese Broccoli

■ 芥蘭菜除老葉及莖部老皮，切約 10 公分洗淨，①料煮開燙 2 分鐘，取出淋沾汁。

■ Remove wilted leaves and hard skin of the stem. Cut broccoli into 4-inch long pieces; rinse. Bring ① to a boil; cook broccoli for 2 minutes. Remove broccoli and serve with seasoning.

生菜 Lettuce

■ 生菜切開洗淨，除硬心部，撕成大片，①料煮開入生菜燙 1 分鐘，取出淋沾汁。

■ Cut lettuce in half then remove the center; tear lettuce into large pieces. Bring ① to a boil; cook lettuce for 1 minute. Remove lettuce and serve with seasoning.

蘆筍 Asparagus

■ 蘆筍修除老皮洗淨，①料煮開放入莖部煮 1 分鐘，再全部放入續燙 1 分鐘，取出切成 2 段，沾汁。

■ Trim off the hard skin and rinse. Bring ① to a boil; place asparagus, stem end first, in boiling water for 1 minute then cook the whole asparagus for another minute. Remove asparagus, cut in half, then serve with seasoning.

沾汁（任選一）：

A 蠔油或醬油 2 大匙（或加蒜末 ½ 大匙）。

B 油 1 大匙炒香蒜末 ½ 大匙，加醬油 2 大匙。

C 沙拉醬 2 大匙。

D 鹽 ⅓ 小匙，胡椒少許（撒在熟蔬菜上）。

如再加撒鰹魚片或炒香芝蔴 1 小匙，可添香味。

SEASONINGS (Choose one of the following):

A 2 T. oyster sauce or 2 T. soy sauce (½ T. minced garlic may be added).

B Heat 1 T. oil then stir-fry ½ T. minced garlic until fragrant; mix in 2 T. soy sauce.

C 2 T. mayonnaise

D ⅓ t. salt and dash of pepper (sprinkle on hot vegetables)

Dried shaved bonito or 1 t. fried sesame seeds may be added for extra flavor.

菠菜 Spinach

■ 菠菜去除枯葉，撕開根部洗淨。①料煮開入菠菜燙 1 分鐘，取出切 5 公分長淋汁，加鰹魚片、芝蔴味更香。

■ Remove wilted leaves and tear off roots; rinse thoroughly. Bring ① to a boil; cook spinach for 1 minute. Remove and cut into 2-inch long pieces. Serve with seasoning. Dried shaved bonito and sesame seeds may be added for extra flavor.

空心菜 Water Convolvulus

■ 空心菜去枯葉，並切除根部洗淨，①料煮開先入莖部煮 1 分鐘，再全部放入續燙 1 分鐘，取出切成 5 公分長淋沾汁。

■ Remove wilted leaves, cut off old stems and rinse. Bring ① to boil; place water convolvulus, stem end first, in boiling water for 1 minute then cook the whole water convolvulus for another minute; remove and cut into 2-inch long pieces. Serve with seasoning.

韭菜 Chinese Leeks

■ 韭菜去枯葉，並切除根部洗淨，①料煮開入韭菜燙 1 分鐘，取出切 5 公分長，撒白芝蔴及魚片淋沾汁。

■ Remove wilted leaves and cut off old stems; rinse. Bring ① to a boil then cook for 1 minute; remove and cut into 2-inch long pieces. Serve with sesame seeds, dried shaved bonito, and seasoning.

鰹魚片豆腐 Bean Curd & Dried Shaved Bonito

■ 豆腐輕輕沖洗，切 1 公分方塊，上置少許蔥、薑末、芝蔴及鰹魚片（見 5 頁），淋醬油即可。

■ Rinse bean curd lightly, being careful not to break it; cut into ½-inch squares. Sprinkle with chopped green onions, minced ginger root, sesame seeds, and dried shaved bonito (see p. 5) then pour soy sauce over the bean curd; serve.

簡易炒蔬菜
Easy Stir-fried Vegetables

2 人份
Serves 2

	蔬菜………… 8 兩（300 公克）			²⁄₃ lb. (300g) vegetables	

①{ 蒜末………………… ½ 大匙
   或葱花………………… 1 大匙

①{ ½ T. minced garlic or 1 T.
     chopped green onions

②{ 鹽………………………… ⅓ 小匙
   胡椒…………………………少許
   麻油（不用亦可）………少許

②{ ⅓ t. salt
     pepper
     sesame oil as desired

四季豆、紅蘿蔔 String Beans & Carrot

■ 四季豆摘除老筋與紅蘿蔔切 5 公分細條，油 1½ 大匙炒香①料，隨入蔬菜略炒，加水 ⅓ 杯及②料，蓋鍋見有水蒸氣冒出再煮 2 分鐘即可。

■ Remove ends and veins on both sides of string beans. Cut string beans and carrot into 2-inch long strips. Heat 1½ T. oil then stir-fry ① until fragrant. Add vegetables and stir-fry briefly. Add ⅓ cup water and ② then cover and cook until steamy; continue to cook for 2 minutes. Remove and serve.

青花菜、義大利瓜 Broccoli & Zucchini
（或去皮絲瓜） (or skinless sponge-gourd)

■ 青花菜切小朵，義大利瓜切片。炒法同「四季豆、紅蘿蔔」。

■ Cut broccoli into flowerets. Slice zucchini. Follow the same procedures as in "String Beans & Carrot."

洋菇、豌豆莢 Mushrooms & Chinese Pea Pods

■ 洋菇、紅蘿蔔均切片，豌豆莢去老筋，炒法同「四季豆、紅蘿蔔」，蓋鍋水蒸氣冒出即可。

■ Slice mushrooms and carrot. Remove both ends and veins on both sides of the Chinese pea pods. Follow the same procedures as in "String Beans & Carrot" to stir-fry vegetables; cover and cook until steamy. Remove and serve.

菠菜   Spinach
（或空心菜） (or water convolvulus)

■ 菠菜洗淨切成 4 段。炒法同「四季豆、紅蘿蔔」，蓋鍋水蒸氣冒出 1 分鐘即可。

■ Rinse spinach then cut into 4 sections. Follow the same procedures as in "String Beans & Carrot" to stir-fry the vegetables; cover and cook until steamy for 1 minute. Remove and serve.

☐ 炒菜用大火可保持菜的翠綠，但需加水以免燒焦，蓋鍋蓋不易油爆，且可在短時間內均勻煮熟。

☐ Using high heat for stir-frying may preserve color of vegetables, but add water when necessary to avoid burning. Covering pan during cooking may prevent spattering and shorten cooking time.

芽菜、包心菜 Bean Sprouts & Cabbage

■ 芽菜洗淨，包心菜、紅蘿蔔切絲或片。炒法同「四季豆、紅蘿蔔」，蓋鍋水蒸氣冒出即可。

■ Rinse bean sprouts, shred or slice cabbage and carrot. Follow the same procedures as in "String Beans & Carrot" to stir-fry vegetables; cover and cook until steamy. Remove and serve.

青梗菜 Bok Choy

■ 青梗菜去除老葉分切成 4-6 瓣，洗淨瀝乾。炒法同「四季豆、紅蘿蔔」。

■ Remove wilted leaves of bok choy then cut each one into four or six pieces; rinse and drain. Follow the same procedures as in "String Beans & Carrot."

青、紅椒、洋葱 Green, Red Peppers & Onion

■ 蔬菜切片或切絲，油 1½ 大匙炒香蒜末（加入切碎豆豉½ 大匙更香），隨入切好蔬菜、②料及水 3 大匙蓋鍋煮 2 分鐘。

■ Slice or shred the vegetables. Heat 1½ T. oil then stir-fry minced garlic until fragrant (½ T. minced fermented black beans may be added for flavor). Add the vegetables, ②, and 3 T. water; cover and cook for 2 minutes. Remove and serve.

芹菜、紅蘿蔔 Celery & Carrot

■ 芹菜去除葉及老筋，切絲，紅蘿蔔亦切絲，炒法同「四季豆、紅蘿蔔」，蓋鍋見水蒸氣冒出即成。

■ Remove old veins of celery; shred the celery and carrot. Follow the same procedures as in "String Beans & Carrot" to stir-fry vegetables; cover and cook until steamy. Remove and serve.

沙拉
Salads

2 人份
Serves 2

各種沙拉汁、沙拉醬做法見 8、9 頁，可任選使用。

To make salad sauces or dressings, see pp. 8, 9. Any salad sauces or dressings may be used as desired.

綜合生菜沙拉 Mixed Lettuce Salad

① 生菜·····························⅓ 個
新鮮洋菇（切片）········ 6 個
洋葱、青椒··············各¼ 個
芹菜·····¼ 杯、番茄·····1 個
「綜合沙拉汁」········ 5 大匙

1/3 head of lettuce
① 6 fresh mushrooms, sliced
1/4 each: onion, green pepper
1/4 c. celery, 1 tomato
5 T. mixed salad dressing

■ 生菜撕成片狀，①料切片或絲，冰涼後淋上沙拉汁。

■ Tear lettuce into pieces and slice or shred ① ; refrigerate. Spread dressing over veagetables when ready to serve.

鷄絲沙拉 Shredded Chicken Salad

生菜·····························⅓ 個
熟雞肉、蝦仁、
蟹肉或洋火腿等 }·············½ 杯
紅蘿蔔絲·····················⅓ 杯
洋葱絲·························3 大匙
炸米粉、粉絲或雲吞皮絲······1 杯
炒熟白芝麻（如無亦可）½ 大匙
「蒜葱沙拉汁」···············5大匙

1/3 head of lettuce
1/2 c. cooked chicken meat, shelled shrimp, crab meat, or ham
1/3 c. shredded carrot
3 T. shredded onion
1 c. deep-fried rice noodles, bean threads, or shredded won ton skin
1/2 T. fried white sesame seeds (optional)
5 T. garlic & onion salad dressing

■ 生菜撕成片狀，鷄肉切絲與全部材料拌勻。食用時淋沙拉汁。

■ Tear lettuce into pieces. Shred chicken meat then mix with the other ingredients. Pour dressing over vegetables when ready to serve.

番茄黃瓜沙拉 Tomato & Cucumber Salad

番茄·····························2 個
小黃瓜·························2 條
「黃瓜沙拉汁」···············5 大匙

2 tomatoes
2 cucumbers
5 T. cucumber salad dressing

■ 番茄選新鮮紅色但不要太軟，洗淨去蒂切塊。小黃瓜間隔去皮切片，略泡水瀝乾。食用時淋上沙拉汁。

■ Choose fresh, red, and hard tomatoes. Remove stems and cut into pieces. Peel cucumbers then slice; briefly soak the slices in water then drain. Mix cucumbers and tomatoes well; pour dressing over them when ready to serve.

綜合水果沙拉 Mixed Fruit Salad

蘋果、桔子（切丁）……… 各 1 個	1 each: tangerine, apple
鳳梨（切丁）………………… ⅓ 杯	⅓ c. diced pineapple
香蕉（去皮切丁）………… 1 條	1 banana, peeled and diced
櫻桃………………………… 4 粒	4 cherries
「蜂蜜沙拉汁」………… 5 大匙	5 T. honey salad dressing

■ 將切好水果置盤，食用時淋上沙拉汁。

■ Dice tangerine and apple. Put all the mixed fruit on a plate then pour dressing over fruit when ready to serve.

鮮菇奶果沙拉 Mushroom & Avocado Salad

捲生菜…………………………… 1 棵	1 head of lettuce
鮮洋菇…………………………… 8 個	8 fresh mushrooms
奶果……………………………… 1 個	1 avocado
洋葱、紅、青椒………切絲各少許	shredded onion, red & green peppers as desired
「醬油沙拉汁」……………… 5 大匙	5 T. soy sauce salad dressing

■ 生菜洗淨撕開葉片鋪盤底。洋菇切片，奶果選已熟透（但不要太軟）去皮切塊，連同青椒、洋葱置生菜上，淋上沙拉汁。

■ Rinse lettuce, tear into pieces. Slice mushrooms. Choose a ripe avocado but not too soft; remove skin and seed then cut into pieces. Put lettuce on a plate; place other vegetables on lettuce. Pour dressing over vegetables when ready to serve.

海菜沙拉 Seaweed Salad

海帶絲或嫩海帶（泡軟）…… 1 杯	1 c. dried shredded seaweed, softened in water
紅、白蘿蔔 ｝………切絲各 ½ 杯 小黃瓜 ｝	½ c. each (shredded): carrot & daikon, cucumber
「梅肉沙拉汁」…………… 5 大匙	5 T. plum salad dressing

■ 海帶泡水 10 分鐘後取出，在沸水中燙 1-2 分鐘撈出，用水冲涼瀝乾（如太長切段），與紅、白蘿蔔絲、黃瓜絲拌勻，食用時淋上沙拉汁。

■ Soak seaweed in water for 10 minutes; remove. Cook seaweed in boiling water for 1-2 minutes; remove, rinse under cold water and drain. Cut seaweed into sections if too long; mix with carrot, daikon, and cucumber. Pour dressing over the vegetables when ready to serve.

沙拉
Salads

2 人份
Serves 2

各種沙拉汁、沙拉醬做法見 8、9 頁，可任選使用。

To make salad sauces and dressings, see pp. 8, 9. Any salad sauces or dressings may be used as desired.

蝦仁洋芋沙拉 Shrimp & Potato Salad

生菜·····4 片	
① 小蝦仁·····½ 杯	
紅蘿蔔、洋芋（切丁）各1個	
靑豆仁·····3 大匙	
鮮洋菇（切片）·····6 個	
「咖哩沙拉醬」·····5 大匙	

- 4 leaves of lettuce
- ① ½ c. small shelled shrimp
- 1 each (diced): potato, carrot
- 3 T. green peas
- 6 fresh mushrooms, sliced
- 5 T. curry salad sauce

■ 生菜洗淨拭乾置盤，①料煮熟與洋菇及沙拉醬拌勻置其上。

■ Rinse lettuce then pat dry; place on a serving plate. Cook ① ; mix with mushrooms and salad sauce then pour on lettuce; serve.

火腿粉絲沙拉 Ham & Bean Threads Salad

粉絲 1 小把 ·····1.5 兩（50 公克）
（或燙豆芽 ·····2 杯）
洋火腿（切絲）·····1 杯
小黃瓜、紅蘿蔔·····切絲各 1 條
「芝麻沙拉醬」·····5 大匙

- 1¾ oz (50g) bean threads or 2 c. bean sprouts
- 1 c. shredded ham
- 1 each (shredded): cucumber, carrot
- 5 T. sesame salad sauce

■ 粉絲用滾水燙煮 1 分鐘，撈出用水冲涼瀝乾，切 10 公分長段與其餘材料及沙拉醬拌勻。冰涼更好吃。

■ Cook bean threads in boiling water for 1 minute; remove and rinse under cold water then drain. Cut bean threads into 4-inch long sections then mix with other ingredients and salad sauce. Best when served cold.

蟹肉包心菜沙拉 Crab Meat & Cabbage Salad

蟹肉或鰹魚罐·····½ 杯
包心菜（切絲）·····2 杯
紫包心菜（切絲）·····1 杯
「茄汁沙拉醬」·····5 大匙

- ½ c. crab meat or tuna
- 2 c. shredded cabbage
- 1 c. shredded red cabbage
- 5 T. ketchup salad sauce

■ 包心菜與紫包心菜切絲冰涼，蟹肉撕成細絲，淋上沙拉醬。

■ Tear crab meat into strips then mix with cabbage and red cabbage; pour on sauce and serve.

□ 洋芋如用微波爐需 5-8 分鐘

□ Potato may be cooked in microwave at high for 5 to 8 minutes.

奶果番茄沙拉 Avocado & Tomato Salad

奶果·························· 1 個	
番茄（切塊）·················· 2 個	
鮮洋菇（切片）················ 6 個	
「芥末沙拉醬」··············· 5 大匙	

1　avocado
2　tomatoes, cut into pieces
6　fresh mushrooms, sliced
5　T. mustard salad sauce

■ 奶果去皮及籽後切塊，全部材料混合，淋上沙拉醬即成。

■ Remove skin and seed of avocado then cut into pieces. Mix all the ingredients then pour on sauce; serve.

葡萄柚沙拉 Grapefruit Salad

葡萄柚························· 1 個	
奶果（切丁）·················· ½個	
杏仁片 4 大匙 ⎱ 或綜合果仁 5 大匙	
葡萄乾 1 大匙 ⎰	
蟹肉·························· ½杯	
「鮮奶油沙拉醬」············· 5 大匙	

1　grapefruit
½ avocado, diced
⎧ 4　T. almond slices
⎩ 1　T. raisin
　(or 5 T. mixed nuts)
½ c. crab meat
5　T. whipping cream
　　salad sauce

■ 葡萄柚切兩半或切 V 字花型，將果肉取出，除去夾層薄皮，撕成小塊，與其餘材料拌勻，裝入葡萄柚內。

■ Cut grapefruit in half or cut deep "v" grooves around it and separate in half. Hollow out grapefruit. Remove white membrane on pulp of grapefruit then tear pulp into small pieces. Mix all the ingredients; put mixture into hollowed grapefruit.

綜合蔬菜沙拉 Mixed Vegetable Salad

芹菜、紅蘿蔔 ⎱ 切絲········各½杯	
青、紅椒 ⎰	
小黃瓜（切絲）················ 1 條	
小紅蘿蔔（去頭尾）············ 6 個	
「綜合沙拉醬」··············· 5 大匙	

½ c. each (shredded):
　　green & red peppers,
　　celery, carrot
1　cucumber, shredded
6　small carrots, remove ends
5　T. mixed salad sauce

■ 青、紅椒絲在滾水中燙 30 秒鐘，撈出。全部材料冰涼後，淋沙拉醬。

■ Blanch green pepper and red pepper in boiling water for 30 seconds; remove and drain. Pour sauce over cold vegetables and serve.

水果拼盤
Assorted Fruit Platters

蘋果⋯⋯⋯⋯⋯⋯⋯⋯ 1 個
鳳梨⋯⋯⋯⋯⋯⋯⋯⋯ 1/4 個
巴西利⋯⋯⋯⋯⋯⋯⋯⋯少許

1 apple
1/4 pineapple
parsley to garnish

4 人份
Serves 4

1 蘋果切半後切除核心，再橫切四片（圖 1），在表皮切∧型刀痕（圖 2），片開表皮至 2/3 處成兔耳型（圖 3），泡鹽水（水 1 杯、鹽 1 小匙）以防變色，約半分鐘取出排盤。

2 鳳梨略修枯葉後，取出皮與核心之間的肉（圖 4、5）切片後，放回原處一片往前一片往後推開（圖 6）。

3 將鳳梨、蘋果片置盤，並以巴西利裝飾即成。

□ 水果種類及其排列，可參考左圖加以變化。

1 Cut apple in half and remove core. Cut each half horizontally in fourths (Fig. 1) then make a "v" cut on the skin of each piece (Fig. 2); peel off skin to ²/₃ to form the shape of rabbit's ear (Fig. 3). Soak apple in salty water, one teaspoon salt dissolved in one cup of water, for about 30 seconds; remove and arrange on a platter.

2 Cut off wilted pineapple leaves. Remove pineapple meat (Figs. 4, 5) then slice. Put sliced pineapple back to its original place; alternately push one slice forward and the next one backward until all slices are arranged as shown (Fig. 6).

3 Arrange the pineapple and apple on a platter and garnish with parsley.

□ Other fruits may be used for different arrangements, see photos at left for reference.

索　引

Index